MIGRATION AND DIASPORA
Exegetical Voices from
Northeast Asian Women

Society of Biblical Literature

International Voices in Biblical Studies

General Editors
Monica J. Melanchthon
Jione Havea

Editorial Board
Eric Bortey Anum
Ida Fröhlich
Hisako Kinukawa
Néstor Míguez
Aliou Niang
Nasili Vaka'uta

Number 6
MIGRATION AND DIASPORA
Exegetical Voices from
Northeast Asian Women

MIGRATION AND DIASPORA
Exegetical Voices from Northeast Asian Women

Edited by
Hisako Kinukawa

SBL Press
Atlanta

Copyright © 2014 by SBL Press

All rights reserved. No part of this work may be reproduced or published in print form except with permission from the publisher. Individuals are free to copy, distribute, and transmit the work in whole or in part by electronic means or by means of any information or retrieval system under the following conditions: (1) they must include with the work notice of ownership of the copyright by the Society of Biblical Literature; (2) they may not use the work for commercial purposes; and (3) they may not alter, transform, or build upon the work. Requests for permission should be addressed in writing to the Rights and Permissions Office, SBL Press, 825 Houston Mill Road, Atlanta, GA 30329, USA.

Library of Congress Cataloging-in-Publication Data

Migration and diaspora : exegetical voices from northeast Asian women / edited by Hisako Kinukawa.
    pages cm. — (Society of Biblical Literature international voices in biblical studies; Volume 6)
  Includes bibliographical references.
   ISBN 978-1-62837-008-9 (paper binding : alk. paper) — ISBN 978-1-62837-009-6 (electronic format) — ISBN 978-1-62837-010-2 (hardcover binding : alk. paper)
  1. Bible—Criticism, interpretation, etc. 2. Christianity—Korea. 3. Emigration and immigration—Religious aspects—Christianity. 4. Asia—Emigration and immigration. 5. Asian diaspora. I. Kinukawa, Hisako, editor.
  BS511.3.M54 2014
  220.6—dc23
                        2014018413

CONTENTS

ABBREVIATIONS..vii

INTRODUCTION...1
Hisako Kinukawa — Center for Feminist Theology and Ministry in Japan

1. Postexilic Jewish Experience and Korean Multiculturalism 3
   Yoon Kyung Lee — Ewha Woman's University, Korea

2. Internal Migrations and Social Justice in Amos and Micah . 19
   Lin Yan — Shenzhen University, People's Republic of China

3. Desiring the Empire: Reading the Book of Esther in Twenty-first Century Korea..27
   Yani Yoo — Methodist Theological University, Korea

4. The Samaritan Woman from the Perspective of a Korean Divorcee..41
   Chanhee Heo — Seoul Women's University, Korea

5. Religious Migration and Diaspora 55
   Hisako Kinukawa — Center for Feminist Theology and Ministry in Japan

CONTRIBUTORS..71

ABBREVIATIONS

BibInt	*Biblical Interpretation*
BRev	*Bible Review*
BTB	*Biblical Theology Bulletin*
CBQ	*Catholic Biblical Quarterly*
CBR	*Currents in Biblical Research*
GTJ	*Grace Theological Journal*
JBL	*Journal of Biblical Literature*
JBQ	*Jewish Bible Quarterly*
JJS	*Journal of Jewish Studies*
JP	*Journal for Preachers*
JPC	*Journal of Psychology and Christianity*
JQR	*Jewish Quarterly Review*
JSOJ	*Journal for the Study of Judaism*
JSOT	*Journal for the Study of the Old Testament*
JSOTSup	*Journal for the Study of the Old Testament Supplement Series*
JTS	*Journal of Theological Studies*
JTSA	*Journal of Theology for Southern Africa*
List	*Listening: Journal of Religion and Culture*
NRSV	New Revised Standard Version
PEQ	*Palestine Exploration Quarterly*
RevExp	*Review and Expositor*
TDNT	*Theological Dictionary of the Old Testament*
VT	*Vetus Testamentum*
WBC	Word Bible Commentary

INTRODUCTION

Hisako Kinukawa

The papers that comprise this volume were presented at the third meeting of Society of Asian Biblical Studies (SABS) held at the Sabah Theological Seminary, Malaysia on June 13–15, 2012 to reflect on the theme of "Migration and Diaspora."

The five writers are women/feminist scholars from Korea, People's Republic of China (PRC), and Japan who locate readings of the biblical text within the framework of their cultures. The three countries are known as recipients of three big world religions, namely Confucianism, Taoism and Buddhism, in addition to their native beliefs and cults. In comparison to the long histories of these religions, Christianity arrived in these countries fairly recently. The three societies have been strongly patriarchal, even though there are variations in the expressions of patriarchy. Women have been among those marginalized/despised/oppressed. Korea and PRC experienced colonization by Japan, which distinguishes between the mentality of being discriminated/marginalized and that of arrogance. This fact has raised sensitive issues between Japan and the two countries.

Besides being multi-religious, the three countries, influenced by globalization, have become increasingly multicultural. We have seen more and more immigrant workers coming as laborers. We have become more conscious of classism and discrimination against different and other ethnicities. Women workers are at the bottom of this ladder of discrimination.

Women/feminist scholars in biblical hermeneutics in this region have raised questions against traditional, male-centered interpretations, offering distinct perspectives based on their experiences of pain, subjugation, and a forced sacrificial philosophy of life. Through their scholarship and activism, they attempt to conscientize women who are still fully immersed in patriarchy/kyriarchy.

The writers do not explicitly identify the methods used to interpret the biblical text, and yet one can discern traces of literary, historical, and postcolonial criticism in their reading of the texts.

Lee Yoon Kyung studies the phenomenon of multiculturalism as it is played out both in postexilic Judah as well as in current Korea. Beginning with a socio-political analysis of the biblical texts, and in conversation with Korean experience, she highlights the plight of "foreign wives" that were brought or came from outside of Korea to marry Korean men but who are seen as the "Others" in Korean society.

Lin Yan takes note of the internal migration phenomena in the huge land of China and then questions the activities of Amos and Micah from a similar perspective. As her title suggests, her interest is also in the execution of social justice in the context of migration and diaspora.

Korean scholar Yani Yoo reads the book of Esther from the perspective of the narrator and his desire. She suggests that the book narrates the story of a few elite people successful with the powers of the time. She sees the tragic ending of the book as a warning against the empire and human greed. Seeing some parallels between the explosive developments in her country and the story, she draws our attention to those in diaspora who have been looked down upon because of their social location and ethnic difference and regarded as cheap labor.

Chanhee Heo does an intertextual reading of the story of the Samaritan woman (John 4:1–12) alongside the novel entitled *My Sweet Home* by Ji-Young Gong, a fellow Korean. Drawing insights from the John text she analyses the main character in the novel and showcases how the woman in the novel finds autonomy and dignity of life through her migration or diasporic experiences in life.

Hisako Kinukawa meets the Syrophoenician woman in Mark as one in diaspora and in parallel to her own Japanese religious migration and sees what transformation the encounter brought Jesus.

Though our social locations are diverse, all of us are committed to finding justice for women in our countries and in our contemporary living through our dialogue with biblical texts. Our struggles for survival in society and our fight for a voice and a space within a patriarchal academy are hard and painfully severe. Despite the resistance, we Asian women/feminist scholars have made efforts to transform the current situation by striving against the discrimination we encounter in our lives as women and as scholars.

We hope we shed some new and distinct light from women/feminist eyes upon the interpretation of the texts on which we have chosen to reflect.

POSTEXILIC JEWISH EXPERIENCE AND KOREAN MULTICULTURALISM

Yoon Kyung Lee

THE HYBRID SITUATION OF KOREA

After the Japanese colonization of Korea (1910–1945) and the Korean War that followed (1950–1953), Korean society created the myth of a "single ethnic nation," by combining extreme nationalism with paternal lineage. In reality, Koreans had already engaged in interracial marriages long before the Japanese occupation of Korea. For instance, the wife of the emperor of the Kaya kingdom (mid-first century CE) was from India, and in the Koryŏ Dynasty (also known as Goryeo Dynasty ruled the Korean Peninsula from 932–1392 CE), kings were forced to marry Mongolian women from the Yuan Dynasty in China (1206–1368 CE). Ancient history of Korea also attests to interracial marriages by the way of naturalization. These marriages, however, were few and the skin color of their descendants was not too different from that of the majority of Koreans.

But the Korean War left an indelible impact on Korean society. American soldiers raped Korean women during the war. The children born as the outcome of these rapes were unwanted and were conspicuous because of their different skin color.[1] Political, economic, and cultural crises have often resulted in attempts to set boundaries and strengthen identity through exclusivism. It is likely, with the experience of the Korean War, that interracial descendants were regarded as a shame to be hidden, for it revealed the weakness of Koreans; that is to say, weakness of the political, economic, and cultural powers of the time.[2]

Since the 1990s, as the result of rapid urbanization of Korea, Korean men who live in rural areas are experiencing difficulty finding wives. Korean women who are pursuing education and employment are not willing to live and work in rural areas. So there has emerged a new trend, which is to look for wives from

---

[1] These children, since the 1950s, were completely ignored. Even though the raped women and their miserable fate were the objects of novels, movies, and dramas, the existence and presence of their descendants were not given full attention. These women were seen as victims and treated with some respect. Yet the descendants of the war were simply treated as unwanted byproducts. These interracial children never spoke in public. They remained long as the invisible and unspoken "other." Some literary and social critics saw this act of violating Korean women by American soldiers as being equivalent to that of violating the patriarchal right of Korean men. Korean society therefore considered interracial children to be non-existent.

[2] In the 1970s, Korean soldiers in turn went to fight the Vietnam War. Like American soldiers, Korean soldiers left many interracial children behind. These Korean-Vietnamese children were also another shameful heritage of Korean exclusivism. Like American soldiers, Korean soldiers did not take responsibility for being fathers to interracial descendants. They were simply byproducts of their sexual contacts.

developing countries such as Vietnam, Uzbekistan, the Philippines, and China. The numbers entering into such unions are growing and such multi-cultural families have become a big social issue. As of 2010, one out of every ten marriages involved a foreign spouse, while the number of children from multiracial families has grown seven-fold from 25,000 in 2006 to 160,000 in 2010. The Korean government has come to the realization that this issue cannot be completely solved only by providing multi-cultural families with materials and resources but by changing the mind-set of native Koreans.

Another issue that confronts the Korean society is that of foreign workers from South East Asia namely, Malaysia, Nepal, Indonesia, Pakistan, and such. As of the year 2011, the numbers of foreign laborers make up about 3% of the entire Korean population. However, these official statistics do not include illegal, undocumented foreign laborers. But workers are still in shortage in Korea. Hundreds and thousands of company owners wait in line to get a visa quota for foreign workers. It means foreign workers are urgently needed for the Korean economy. The growing numbers of foreign workers means that Koreans now have to deal with many other issues that accompany them. For instance, Ansan, an industrial city south of Seoul, is a massive center for foreign laborers. Burglary, rape, counterfeit registration cards, or fabrication of documents for false marriages by foreign laborers are rampant. At the same time, poor working conditions for foreign workers such as physical abuse and withholding of wages have emerged as social issues revealing ugly aspects of Korean society.

Koreans and Korean society are now confronted with unprecedented social, political, and cultural effects of "multiculturalism." Koreans today hesitate to speak of being a people of "a single ethnic nation." The phrase, "a single ethnic nation" remains a myth of the past. In this paper, I'd like to focus on the issue of "foreign wives" in Korean society. Korean society in large has gradually recognized that foreign wives are the "Other" but still a part of the Koreans. In analyzing the issue of "foreign wives and their children," this paper turns to the similar historical incident in Yehud of the Persian period. By examining the biblical incident as highlighted by the prohibition against foreign wives by Ezra and Nehemiah, I will argue below that the aspiration for "a pure ethnicity" and "an original religion" cannot help but fail, and offer no resolutions to the situation in Korea.

THE HYBRID SITUATION OF YEHUD IN THE PERSIAN PERIOD

It is not easy to dismiss the commandment of prohibition and cancellation of marriages with foreign wives as suggested by Ezra and Nehemiah (Ezra 9–10; Neh 13). Within the context of Korea's growing multiculturalism, these seemingly xenophobic passages are confusing to the ordinary reader. The prohibition of foreign wives in Ezra and Nehemiah seems to be a radically religious act based on the spiritual aspiration to keep the purity of the Jewish religion. The question that arises then, "was it necessary for the Jewish leaders to decree so violent an injunction with and for the sake of religion?"

THE CONSTITUENTS OF YEHUD IN THE PERSIAN PERIOD: MAKING A MYTH

The origins of Israel lie within an assembly of a multitude of different ethnic groups. When they escaped from Egypt, "a mixed multitude went up also with them" (KJV, Ex 12:38). Also, Moses urged the Israelites to confess that "My father was a wandering Aramean" (Deut 26:5). Even more, Abraham was originally from the city of Ur, Sumer. Abraham himself had a son from an Egyptian woman, Hagar. God protected her and her son. Her ethnicity was not an issue at all. It is clear, however, that there were strong oppositions against Philistine/Canaanite women. For instance, Abraham and his wife Sarah wanted no Canaanite daughter-in-law (Gen 24:3, 27; 27:46), Likewise, Isaac commanded Jacob not to marry a Philistine woman (Gen 28:1). Esau found a second wife from the tribe of Ishmael to please his parents, although he had already married a Canaanite woman (Gen 28:8). There were certainly objections against marriage to Philistine/Canaanite women. But this category is consistent with the boundary set for "Total Destruction" (חֵרֶם *herem*) in the Holy War manual. That is, the prohibition of a certain ethnic group for marriage is definitely limited to those who were in their adjacent territories.

The nation "Israel" was not composed of a single ethnic group. In the Bible, interracial marriages were widespread. Joseph married Asenath, the daughter of Potiphera, priest of On (Gen 41:45). Moses married a Cushite woman. Although Aaron and Miriam opposed this marriage, God allowed this (Num 12). But then, there is an account such as Num 25, according to which Israelites were having sexual relationships with Moabite women and joined them in offering sacrifices to their gods. As a result of this contact, 24,000 Israelites died. But, in stark contrast to this incident, the two daughters-in-law of Naomi were Moabites (Ruth 1:4), one of whom became a maternal ancestor to King David. Therefore, in comparing these two accounts related to Moabite women, the reason why God punished Israelites was definitely related not to the women's ethnicity, but to their idolatry. King David himself also married a Geshur woman by whom he sired Abshalom.[3] In short, reflecting the history prior to the Persian period, interracial marriage was not encouraged but neither was it prohibited.

Against this historical tradition, it seems odd that all of a sudden in the Persian period the complete ban on interracial marriage was proclaimed. Why did Ezra and Nehemiah proclaim such a ban? Did they attempt to establish an ethnically pure Yehud? In fact, the postexilic Yehud was not a racially unified

---

[3] Geshur was a part of the northern part of Bashan (Deut 3:14; 2 Sam 15:8).

state. It rather consisted of a variety of peoples in terms of ethnicity.[4] Nehemiah reported that there were groups who were racially different from the Yehudites. Reading the accounts of Nehemiah, it seems that there were only two racially different groups in the Persian period: Jews and non-Jews. However, the problem was not that simple at all. We need to examine the two groups in depth.

First, the Yehudite group was not a single entity. Although the Yehudite group was racially one internally, it was classified into two subgroups and one discriminated against the other. One is those returning from exile. This group was called "those who came up" (Ezra 2:59; Neh 7:61) הָעֹלִים , "those who had returned from exile" (Ezra 6:21) הַשָּׁבִים מֵהַגּוֹלָה , and "those who came from the captivity" (Ezra 3:8) הַבָּאִים מֵהַשְּׁבִי . Usually, the returnees seem to have taken the high power in every aspect, that is, religious, political, and economic status. But even the returnee group was not a unified one. The returnees had internal conflicts and divisions within themselves. For instance, amidst the priestly returnees, three priestly family groups could not prove their genealogical lineage, and so their priestly status was deprived (Ezra 2:62–63). The other Yehudite group within the postexilic Yehud was the native local people, who were not taken into captivity in Babylon. These people must have been the majority population of Yehud, who belonged to the lower class in terms of their religious, political and economic status. The conflictual relationship between the native and returnee Yehudite groups was particularly noticed in Third Isaiah.[5] Thus, a single-unified-essential Yehudite community of the postexilic Yehud is evidently all myth and fantasy.

The second group of non-Jews was called "the peoples of the land" (לְעַמֵּי הָאָרֶץ) (Neh 10:30, MT 10:31).[6] This phrase signifies that many peoples of different ethnicities lived together with Yehudites. We need to particularly pay

---

[4] For the study of various terminologies for different groups in Ezra and Nehemiah, see Joel Weinberg, *Citizen-Temple Community* (Sheffield: Sheffield Academic, 1992).

[5] P. D. Hanson, *The Dawn of the Apocalyptic: The Historical and Sociological Roots of Jewish Apocalyptic Eschatology* (Philadelphia: Fortress, 1975); Jon Berquist reads the entire Third Isaiah as the actions and reactions between the natives and the priestly immigrants. See his book, *Judaism in Persia's Shadow* (Minneapolis, Minn.: Fortress, 1995), 75–77; Walter Brueggemann also connects the inclusiveness of Third Isaiah to the reforms of Ezra and Nehemiah. See his book, *Isaiah 40–66* (Louisville: Westminster John Knox, 1998), 169; In contrast, Claus Westermann claims that Third Isaiah was written prior to Ezra and Nehemiah, suggesting that they had no relation at all to each other. See his commentary, *Isaiah 40–66*, The Old Testament Library, (Philadelphia: Westminster, 1969), 295–96; J. Blenkinsopp interprets Isaiah 56:1–18 not as a counteraction against Ezra and Nehemiah. See his commentary, *Isaiah 56–66*, AB 19B, (New York: Doubleday, 2003), 142–43.

[6] For the study of the term of "the people of the land," see L. S. Fried, "The *'am ha'ares* in Ezra 4:4 and Persian Administration," in *Judah and the Judeans in the Persian Period*, eds. O. Lipschits and M. Oeming; (Winona Lake, Ind.: Eisenbrauns, 2006), 123–45.

attention to the Samaritans who are conventionally regarded as interracial people since the Fall of Samaria by the Assyrians in 722. In contrast to our prejudice, which is perhaps influenced by the accounts of the New Testament, the Samaritans were not regarded as the "Other" in the Persian Era. The governor of Samaria had a marital relationship with the high priest family of Jerusalem. According to Nehemiah, a daughter of Sanballat, governor of Samaria, married one of the grandsons of the high priest Eliashib (Neh 13:28). Based on this account, it is inferred that the Samaritans were not excluded but included in the list of the possible mates for the high priest family. That is, the Samaritans were considered as possible spouse candidates for the high priestly family in the Persian period. We have two more extra-biblical references to the Sanballat family. One reference is found in Josephus (*Ant.* 11.7.2),[7] who provides us with extra information about Sanballat. According to Nehemiah, Sanballat was a Horonite and a local power elite, but Josephus records that Sanballat, was a Cutheam, who was sent to Samaria by Darius. Sanballat was a royal imperial administrator similar to Nehemiah. Josephus also gives the specific names of these characters mentioned in Nehemiah. The name of Sanballat's daughter was Nicaso. The name of the grandson of high priest Eliashib who Nicaso married was Manasseh. There appears to be a difference between Nehemiah and Josephus. According to Josephus, Manasseh was a brother of Eliashib, not a grandson.[8] Even more significant is that Josephus states that Sanballat entered into this matrimonial relationship for political reasons, which is to continue good relations with the power elite group of Yehud.

Another historical source that informs us of the Sanballat family is the *Elephantine papyri,* which records Sanballat as having two sons, Delaiah and Shelemiah.[9] The Jews of Elephantine asked for the help of Sanballat's sons in rebuilding their Temple. Based on this information, it is assumed that Samaria and her authorities were regarded as highly as the Jerusalem authorities and as Yahweh worshippers by the Elephantine Jews. This record also suggests that the

---

[7] "Now when John had departed this life, his son Jaddua succeeded in the high priesthood. He had a brother, whose name was Manasseh. Now there was one Sanballat, who was sent by Darius, the last king [of Persia], into Samaria. He was a Cutheam by birth; of which stock were the Samaritans also. This man knew that the city Jerusalem was a famous city, and that their kings had given a great deal of trouble to the Assyrians, and the people of Celesyria; so that he willingly gave his daughter, whose name was Nicaso, in marriage to Manasseh, as thinking this alliance by marriage would be a pledge and security that the nation of the Jews should continue their good-will to him."

[8] The reason for this difference seems to be derived from Josephus's misplacing Sanballat in the reign of Darius III Codomannus (c. 380–330 BCE), so that Josephus possibly confused the biblical Sanballat with one of his successors, possibly Sanballat II or Sanballat III.

[9] This information is from TAD A4.7 Cowley 30. Bezalel Porten, et al. *The Elephantine Papyri in English: Three Millennia of Cross-Cultural Continuity and Change* (Leiden: Brill, 1996), 146.

division between Samaria and Jerusalem was not noted by those who lived in Diaspora perhaps because such a division was not yet firmly rooted at least during this period of time.[10] Despite the claim that the split was already made long before the exile,[11] and based on the pieces of information provided by Josephus and the Elephantine papyri, it can be inferred that the most evident proof of the origin of anti-Samaritanism is found in the opposition and rejection by Ezra and Nehemiah. Before the accounts of Ezra and Nehemiah we have no record or even indication of pre-exilic Judah treating Samaria and Samaritans as non-Israelites or non-Yahweh worshippers.

Nehemiah also identified Tobiah as a non-Jew and as an anti-Jewish opponent and as an Ammonite. Yet, like the Sanballat family, the Tobiad family also had matrimonial relationships with a Yehudite power elite group. Tobiah's son Jehohanan married the daughter of Meshullam the son of Berechiah (Neh 6:18), one of the builders of the Jerusalem wall (Neh 3:3, 30). Assuming from the fact that Meshullam's genealogy was traced back to his grandfather, his family was definitely one of the leading families amidst the returnees. Even more, Eliashib, the same high priest who was married into the Sanballat family, rented a room in the Temple for Tobiah, so he could house his valuables in Jerusalem.

Josephus too testifies to the Tobiad family (*Ant.* 12.154–236). Surprisingly, Josephus portrayed a descendant of Tobiah the Ammonite as an ideal diasporic figure. In addition to Josephus, the later history of the Tobiad family was recorded in 2 Macc 3:11[12] and in the Zenon papyri.[13] The extra-biblical accounts all point to the influence and power of the Tobiad family, which exerted strong power in Ptolemaic Palestine, long after the time of Nehemiah. The Tobiad family had strong connections with Jerusalem until the period reflecting the context of 2 Maccabees and the Zenon papyri.

As the above information shows, Ezra and Nehemiah set a very narrow and rigid boundary for what it requires to be a Jew. The conditions and criteria of

---

[10] See this position in Lester L. Grabbe, "Betwixt and Between: The Samaritans in the Hasmonean Period," in *Second Temple Studies III: Studies in Politics, Class, and Material Culture,* eds. Philip R. Davies and John M. Halligan, (London: Sheffield Academic, 2002), 202–17.

[11] Even within the theory of a pre-exilic origin of the split, there were different identifications for the Samaritans. There are different suppositions such as "proto-Samaritan," "descendants from the ten tribes of Israel," "the remnant of Ephraim and Manasseh," "true descendants of the *B'nay Yisrael*" or "a Persian-Hellenistic origin as dissident priests." Cf. Ingrid Hjelm, "What do Samaritans and Jews Have in Common? Recent Trends in Samaritan Studies," *CBR* 3.1 (2004): 13–14.

[12] "The high priest explained that there were deposits for widows and orphans, and some was the property of Hyrcanus, son of Tobias, a man who occupied a very high position" (2 Macc 3:10–11a).

[13] Campbell C. Edgar, *Zenon Papyri in the University of Michigan Collection* (Ann Arbor: University of Michigan Press, 1931).

being a real Jew was racial lineage, regardless of one's religious affiliation. However, the policy of Ezra and Nehemiah did not last long, inferring from the fact that both the Sanballat and the Tobiad survived the xenophobic policy and in fact, prospered long after. In short, the postexilic Yehud was a hybrid society.

THE AMBIVALENCE OF THE WALL

The first and foremost mission of Nehemiah was to build the wall around Jerusalem.[14] In the communication between King Artaxerxes and Nehemiah, the burned wall and its ruined gates were revealed as the primary concern (Neh 2:1–5). Because the conversation is couched in Nehemiah's emotional speech, it is easily overlooked that the rebuilding project was indeed more than a religiously aspired work. It is of great interest that King Artaxerxes sent Nehemiah with army officers and cavalry to help him confront the opposition from Sanballat, Tobiah, Geshem and others (Neh 2:19; 4:7; 6:1, etc.). Nehemiah could protect the building project with armed personnel (Neh 4:7–23) and could finish it in fifty-two days (Neh 6:15). Considering the military and financial support from the Persian Empire, Berquist is right in suggesting that the fortification project of the Jerusalem wall was part of the imperial policy of intensifying its vast territory.[15] The more serious effect of the fortification project was the increased division of the internal Yehudite community.

> Those who will live within the walls of the restored city include the priests, the temple servants, merchants, goldsmiths, perfumers, and others—clearly the upper classes of Yehudite society. The rebuilt city exists for the urban elite and their cohorts from Persia; the outlying, unprotected countryside remains for the poorer inhabitants of the land.[16]

---

[14] There are debates on the extent of Nehemiah's wall. According to the minimalists, the wall was restricted to the City of David. In contrast, the maximalists claim the wall was extended to the southwestern hill. Regarding the archaeological issues of Nehemiah's wall, see Israel Finkelstein, "Jerusalem in the Persian (and early Hellenistic) Period and the Wall of Nehemiah," *JSOT* 32/4 (2008): 507.

[15] Berquist, *Judaism*, 111–16. Likewise, O. Margalith also proposes a similar proposition that Jerusalem was a "Persian frontier-post against the Greek." See his article, "The Political Background of Zerubbabel's Mission and the Samaritan Schism," *VT* 41 (1991): 312. In contrast, Grabbe maintains that Nehemiah rebuilt the wall for internal reasons such as social control, and not for defense. See Lester L. Grabbe, "'They Shall Come Rejoicing to Zion'—Or Did They? The Settlement of Yehud in the Early Persian Period," in *Exile and Restoration Revisited: Essays on the Babylonian and Persian Periods in Memory of Peter R. Ackroyd*, eds. G. N. Knoppers and L. L. Grabbe with D. Fulton, (New York: T&T Clark, 2009), 121.

[16] Berquist, *Judaism*, 114.

The wall was primarily rebuilt to prevent non-imperial peoples from crossing over. But, simultaneously, the wall became a social, economic, and racial wall, so that the lower class of Yehudites and non-Jews had no access to enter and to mix up. Yet, despite its grand appearance, the wall is fundamentally ambivalent and in-between. The gates of the wall are always in liminal space, both open and closed at the same time. There are people who would want to open but, simultaneously, there are those who resist. The seemingly secure wall divides the rich/elite/leading Jews and the poor/native/subjective Jews; it separates the Jews and non-Jews. It is deemed to exist for nonexistence. The elite group who tried hard to keep their boundary by fortifying the wall under the Persian Empire was in the same fate as the rest of the people, for they also strived to cross the imperial bureaucratic borderline. Thus, the fortified wall never functioned as a clear-cut boundary to separate the elite Yehudites from the rest surrounding them. The wall was always vulnerable to be breached. As Josephus and the papyri of Elephantine and Zenon inform, even with the fortified physical wall, the political, economic, and matrimonial relationship of the Jerusalemites with Samaria and Ammon continued long after the period of Ezra and Nehemiah.

PROHIBITION AGAINST INTERRACIAL MARRIAGE

In this context and against this situation, Ezra and Nehemiah went further to prevent and to cancel all interracial marriages completely. As noted above, such a violent action at large had never been enforced in the history of Israel. Moreover, Israel had never claimed to be a single ethnic nation. Rather, it came from "a mixed multitude" (Exod 12:38).[17] And now in returning, Ezra and Nehemiah found that Yehud was composed of a variety of peoples. But then why did Ezra and Nehemiah enforce their bigotry to the extreme? What did Ezra and Nehemiah aim to attain through their policy and strategy of "cleansing and purifying the local face of the nation"?[18]

IMPURITY

Who were the foreign wives? Although they seem to have been racially different, there is the possibility that the women who were forced to divorce were not ethnically of a different race, but the native Yehudite who had no experience of the exile.[19] But this suggestion is, it seems, not valid. The text that "half of their

---

[17] "A mixed multitude" (KJV NASB, RSV); "many other people" (NIV).

[18] Frantz Fanon, *The Wretched of the Earth* (New York: Grove Press, 1963), 83.

[19] This suggestion has been made by scholars such as Lester Grabbe, *A History of the Jews and Judaism in the Second Temple Period, vol. 1: Yehud: A History of the Persian Province of Judah* (New York: T&T Clark, 2004), 285–88, 313–16; Tamara C. Eskenazi and Eleanore P. Judd, "Marriage to a Stranger in Ezra 9–10," in *Second Temple Studies II: Temple and Community in the Persian Period,* eds. Tamara C. Eskenazi and

children spoke the language of Ashdod, and they could not speak the language of Judah, but the language of each people (Neh 13:24)" implies that foreign wives were literally and racially foreigners rather than the native Yehudite women. Then, why did foreign women marry repatriated men? In response to this question, scholars employing Merton's "hypergamy theory"[20] explain that the native local women exchanged their land to "marry up" into the ranks of the returning elites.[21] This theory seems somewhat plausible in that the texts of Ezra and Nehemiah never referred to the case that the repatriated women married the local native men. But this theory cannot explain why the power elite group of Jerusalem married with the Sanballat and the Tobiad families. Moreover, in case of the Tobiad family, Tobiah's son married a daughter of an elite Jewish family.

Why, then, did Ezra and Nehemiah prohibit intermarriage? Before surveying the possible propositions, we need to compare the two accounts of Ezra and Nehemiah. Generally, Ezra 9–10 and Neh 13:23–31 are considered to be two separate accounts regarding the same incident.[22] But the two have different foci. Ezra seems to focus more on the leading class in dealing with this issue (Ezra 9:1–2). Thus, Ezra primarily criticized the intermarriages of the priestly and Levitical classes. By contrast, Nehemiah approaches this issue in a manner similar to the critique against Solomon. By focusing on marriage to women from Israel's traditional enemies, Nehemiah relates mixed marriage with the issue of keeping their traditional religion and culture (for instance, language). Nehemiah sets the Sanballat family as an example case (13:28). Since he names Sanballat, we can assume that Nehemiah's prohibition of intermarriage did not have a single-minded goal, for instance, to keep the traditional values and purity of religion. Considering the different foci of Ezra and Nehemiah with the same policy, it is assumed that such a violent enforcement did not consist of a single, isolated cause, but instead led to a complex chain of crises.

Thus far, scholars explain the prohibition of intermarriage with a religious cause. Ezra and Nehemiah prohibited intermarriage based on the Deuteronomic

---

Kent H. Richards, (Sheffield: Sheffield Academic, 1994), 266–85; Bob Becking, "On the Identity of the 'Foreign' Women in Ezra 9–10," in *Exile and Restoration Revisited,* eds. G. N. Knoppers and L. L. Grabbe with D. Fulton, (London: T&T Clark, 2009), 31–49.

[20] R. K. Merton, "Intermarriage and Social Structure: Fact and Theory," *Psychiatry* 4 (1941): 361–74.

[21] Gale Y. Yee, *Poor Banished Children of Eve: Woman as Evil in the Hebrew Bible* (Minneapolis, Minn.: Fortress, 2003), 144; Daniel L. Smith-Christopher, "The Mixed Marriage Crisis in Ezra 9–10 and Nehemiah 13: A Study of the Sociology of the Post-exilic Judean Community," in *Second Temple Studies 2: Temple and Community in the Persian Period,* eds. T. C. Eskenazi and K. H. Richards, (Sheffield: Sheffield Academic, 1994), 261; D. L. Smith-Christopher, *A Biblical Theology of Exile* (Minneapolis, Minn.: Fortress, 2002), 153–55.

[22] But D. L. Smith-Christopher proposes the texts of Ezra and of Nehemiah are two separate accounts. "The Mixed Marriage Crisis in Ezra," 244.

legal stipulation to preserve racial and religious purity (Deut 7:3–4).[23] In hearing the report of the priestly and Levitical members' intermarriages, Ezra's reaction was quite dramatic: "I rent my garments and my mantle, and pulled hair from my head and beard, and sat appalled" (RSV, Ezra 9:3). This was followed by other religious actions of kneeling down and praying with stretched hands toward the heaven (Ezra 9:5). Yet, another reason behind this action is suggested. That is, the postexilic returnee community prohibited intermarriage because of economic and political reasons.[24] Berquist claims that Ezra focused on the leading elite classes of Jerusalem for entirely economic reasons. By prohibiting interracial marriage, they could prevent aliens from inheriting property. In concert, Ezra and Nehemiah had a political intention to stop the Samaritans and the Ammonites exerting political power in Jerusalem; "It could produce opportunities for foreign officials to exercise undue influence on Yehud's internal matters (Neh 13:28)."[25] Thus, foreign women, all of a sudden, were confronted with the situation of returning home with children but without any financial support. The most miserable fact is that they had no opportunity to reunite with their family. Even without any condition, the families were set apart forever. Although scholars have thus far considered the policy of prohibition of interracial marriages from religious, economic, and political aspects, this issue should also be examined from a socio-political perspective.

COUNTERING REGRESSIVE NATIVISM

As a socio-political phenomenon, the policy of prohibition of interracial marriages seems similar to "regressive nativism." According to post-colonial theory, "nativism" is a term that expresses "the desire to return to indigenous practices and cultural forms as they existed in pre-colonial society."[26] By restricting the ethnic boundary to the smallest group, Ezra and Nehemiah seem to have tried to restore the postexilic Yehud to the pre-exilic state of Israel. In order to recover the pre-exilic status, Ezra and Nehemiah took steps to strengthen hostility and intense opposition to an internal minority such as foreign wives and contributed to internal rivalry against Sanballat and Tobiah. Ezra and Nehemiah used this strategy of separating the "Other" and solidifying repatriated Yehudite men. Ezra-Nehemiah attempted to establish their Yehudite identity by setting strict boundaries and dividing the class layers much more

---

[23] However, some scholars deny that the Deuteronomic law never authorizes the action taken by Ezra and Nehemiah. L. Batten, *Ezra and Nehemiah*, ICC, (Edinburgh: T&T Clark, 1980), 331; J. Blenkinsopp, *Ezra-Nehemiah*, Old Testament Library, (London: SCM, 1988), 176; H. G. M. Williamson, *Ezra, Nehemiah*, WBC, (Waco, Tex.: Word, 1985), 130–32.
[24] Berquist, *Judaism*, 118–19.
[25] Berquist, *Judaism*, 118.
[26] B. Ashcroft, G. Griffiths, and H. Tiffin, *Post-Colonial Studies: The Key Concepts* (New York: Routledge, 2000), 159.

sharply and deeply even within Yehudites, just as in the case of the priestly families. The strategy to define the highest priestly class as narrowly as possible enforces the class division within Yehudites. In so doing, Ezra and Nehemiah created an "Other" within Yehudites. Simultaneously, Ezra and Nehemiah rejected the half-Jews such as Sanballat and Tobiah. Although the primary cause of objection by Nehemiah was political due to the internal power struggles in the Persian Empire, Nehemiah craftily identified Sanballat and Tobiah as non-Jews by repeatedly calling them the Samaritans and the Ammonites, respectively. Before the enforcement of the policy of division by Nehemiah, Jews and these (half-) Jews had close contacts, including matrimonial relationships. This fact implies that their ethnic identity—regardless of their ethnicity—was not an issue at all. Nevertheless, Ezra and Nehemiah expelled foreign wives by regarding them as possible agents of pollution.

However, the divisive policy of Ezra and Nehemiah was not welcomed unanimously. Despite the radically violent reformation, there are oppositional flows against the policy of Ezra and Nehemiah. For instance, by identifying the priestly groups affiliated with the first builders of the temple as the Zadokites, Hanson proposes that the Levitical priests who remained in the land were gradually isolated from the temple service after the Zadokite priestly family returned from exile and took control, and conflicts developed between these two groups.[27] In a similar vein, Mary Douglas suggests that Leviticus and Numbers contain a counter response to the exclusivist policy of Ezra and Nehemiah.[28] More frequently, it is pointed out that Third Isaiah is the most representative counter-action theologian.[29] Isaiah 56:1–8, in which foreigners, along with the eunuchs, are included in the general assembly of God, is generally interpreted as the opposing theological position to Ezra and Nehemiah.[30] In stark contrast to Ezra and Nehemiah's xenophobic policy, Third Isaiah presents a totally opposing viewpoint toward foreigners:

> And foreigners who bind themselves to the LORD to serve him, to love the name of the LORD, and to worship him, all who keep the Sabbath without desecrating it and who hold fast to my covenant—these I will bring to my

---

[27] Thus Hanson reads Isa 63:7–64:11 as the Levitical priestly classes' critique. Hanson, *The Dawn*, 95.

[28] Mary Douglas, "Responding to Ezra: The Priests and the Foreign Wives," *BibInt* 10/1 (2002): 1–23.

[29] For the dating of Third Isaiah, there exist diverse opinions. Among them, there are scholars who date Third Isaiah as a contemporary of (Koenen) and later than Nehemiah (Watts). For instance, John D. W. Watts dates Third Isaiah to 435 BCE. See his commentary, *Isaiah 34–66*, WBC 25, (Waco, Tex.: Word Books, 1987).

[30] Pauritsch, Sehmsdorf, Donner, and Lau. Recited from B. S. Childs, *Isaiah*, Old Testament Library, (Louisville: Westminster John Knox, 2001), 457. Clinton E. Hammock, "Isaiah 56:1–8 and the Redefining of the Restoration Judean Community," *BTB* 30 (2000): 46–57; John D. W. Watts, *Isaiah 34–66*, 249.

holy mountain and give them joy in my house of prayer. Their burnt offerings and sacrifices will be accepted on my altar; for my house will be called a house of prayer for all nations (56:6–7).

As hinted above, difference in ethnicity is not a problem in itself; rather, the issue is whether foreigners are united with Jews in terms of religious fidelity to Yawhism. Anyone who keeps the Sabbath law is welcomed into the Assembly of God. According to Third Isaiah, the identity of the people of God is not based upon racial and ethnic lineage but on one's voluntary decision to accept the God of Israel and his/her loyalty to divine commandments. Actually, this criterion seems just natural and should not surprise our modern mind. But this is a radical stipulation, which goes against the legal tradition.

Deuteronomy 23:1–9 lists the types of people who are to be excluded from the assembly of Israel. In this list, eunuchs and illegitimate children and their descendants are excluded. In addition, this list specifically refers to the Ammonites and the Moabites as ethnic groups who are excluded. But in the case of the Edomites, their descendants can be included only after the tenth generation. This Deuteronomic stipulation seems likely to have provided a proof-text for the radical anti-foreigner policy of Ezra and Nehemiah. In contrast, Third Isaiah gives a totally opposite stipulation and provides the rationale for why foreigners and eunuchs are to be included in the assembly of Israel. Both Third Isaiah and Ezra/Nehemiah had experienced the exile and lived under Persian colonial control. However, they proclaimed totally opposing stipulations toward foreigners. Why did they present totally opposing blueprints for the future? Despite being deeply rooted in the same religious tradition, they interpreted their legal tradition differently. According to Deut 23:1ff, as noted above, the Ammonites/Moabites and the Edomites were treated differently. The former had no chance of being included until the tenth generation, while the latter by the third generation. But as the narrative of Ruth and the later episodes[31] show, the Israelites and the Moabites were in good relations. This indicates that the Deuteronomic law was not practiced in reality. Moreover, blood purity was already contaminated long before the time of Ezra and Nehemiah. The attempt to pursue and restore the pure blood lineage by expelling foreign wives is an unattainable venture. To return to the pre-exilic state and status is a mission impossible. Ezra and Nehemiah's "regressive nativism" in order to set up an exclusive identity produced the "Other." In so doing, they believed that they could consolidate the inner circle of the repatriate community. However, history proves that any political party or group who stress

---

[31] David made a refuge for his parents in Mizpah, Moab, for his grandmother, Ruth, was a Moabite (2 Sam 21:3–4).

"ethnic purity" by violently producing the "Other" end up failing their missions.[32]

BIBLICAL RESPONSE TO THE KOREAN MULTI-CULTURAL CONTEXT

Like the Persian Yehud, Korea has now been on the threshold of a multicultural society, specifically in terms of ethnicity. Confronted by the unprecedented social issue of multiculturalism, Korea has now been through a situation similar to postexilic Yehud. Like the Persian Yehud, Korean society also has a double strategy within which are multiple layers. Korean government promotes "globalization" by way of frequently featuring successful Korean businessmen/women in foreign countries and dubbing them as global Koreans. With the ideology of globalization, the Korean government has officially promoted "English immersion education" in schools, and has passed the Free Trade Agreement with the USA, despite tremendous opposition by Koreans, fearing possible economic and political subjugation to the USA. On the superficial level, such globalization strategy seems to be consistent with multiculturalism. But under the name of globalization, those who belong to the top tax bracket and speak English are different from those who belong to the bottom tax bracket and whose children speak their mother tongue. Korean government and local municipalities have initiated various programs to support foreign wives such as providing Korean language courses and social adaptation programs. Yet, thus far, the Korean approach is typically for foreign wives to learn Korean and to adapt themselves to Korean society, rather than encouraging foreign wives to teach their mother tongue to their children. Their mother tongue is overlooked and is even considered as the one to be forgotten.

In Persian Yehud, Nehemiah enforced the cancellation of intermarriage with the Ammonites and the Moabites on the grounds that their children spoke their mothers' tongue. Furthermore, Nehemiah likened foreign wives to agents of religious impurity. Due to foreign wives, according to the logic of Nehemiah, Yehudite men had surrendered to idolatry. Within Persian Yehud, only the small bracket of the repatriate, elite Yehudite group is given the full privilege to be a real Jew. Half-Jews or alien residents or naturalized Jews were not given a chance to be assimilated. In the Persian Empire, these people were the colonized of the colonized peoples. The strategy of Ezra and Nehemiah to consolidate that small bracket of the so-called real Jews was opposed from within. Third Isaiah

---

[32] In our recent history, Hitler's policy of "a pure Aryan race" led the world into chaos. In ancient times, the Ptolemies who wished to maintain their Greek heritage in Egypt seemed to prefer to marry among themselves. For about 300 years, Cleopatra VII was the first and last member of the Ptolemaic line who was able to speak Egyptian.

opposed the essentialism of ethnicity. As noted above, according to Third Isaiah, tradition and community are continued not by ethnic purity but by religious purity. Under the name of Yahwism all constituents of Persian Yehud should be unified and assembled. The door is open to anyone who is willing to be obedient and faithful to Yawhism. Although both had common tradition and religion, Ezra/Nehemiah and Third Isaiah had different stances for the future of Persian Yehud. The slight but significant difference between Ezra/Nehemiah and Third Isaiah was derived from their viewpoint on whether to include or to exclude foreigners who are faithful to Yawhism. Whose blueprint was actualized in history? The Ammonites did survive until the end of Ptolemaic control over Palestine. The Samaritans did survive until the time of Jesus and even today.

On the threshold of entering into multiculturalism, Korean society has gradually unloaded the myth of "a single ethnic nation" and is now struggling to deal with the issues of a multicultural family. Korea has enforced the "Support Law of Multicultural Family" since 2008. The success of this law is totally dependent on the mind of law enforcement. When the two terms, "globalization" and "multiculturalism," continue to signal two different policies in parallel, the wall to divide and separate Koreans is hard to tear down. In all ages, the wall—whether physical or metaphorical—collides with the colonizer and is designed to protect the imperial boundary and the small bracket of the colonized elites. However, the wall is vulnerable and ambivalent, for there are always those who try to make a breach. The wall, as always, is fated to be breached by a torrent of profound multiculturalism. As Ezra and Nehemiah have shown, the strategy to create conflict by stressing identity and giving rise to the "Other" is deemed unfit for starting up a new nation. In retrospect, their strategy of making the Samaritans the "Other" split the postexilic Yehud forever. Only when Jesus came did the issue of pure and impure blood reopen, and a remedy was found to be able to go forward. Should we reflect biblical history in the attempt to create a future history?

BIBLIOGRAPHY

Bartlett, John R. "Nehemiah's Wall *PEQ* 140 /2 (2008): 77–78.
Bedford, Peter R. "Diaspora: Homeland Relations in Ezra–Nehemiah." *VT* 52/2 (2002): 147–65.
Berquist Jon L. *Judaism in Persia's Shadow*. Minneapolis, Minn.: Fortress, 1995.
———. *Approaching Yehud: New Approaches to the Study of the Persian Period*. Atlanta: Society of Biblical Literature, 2008.
Blenkinsopp, Joseph. *Judaism the First Phase: The Place of Ezra and Nehemiah in the Origins of Judaism*. Grand Rapids: Eerdmans, 2009.
Cataldo, Jeremiah. "Persian Policy and the Yehud Community during Nehemiah." *JSOT* 28/2 (2003): 240–52.
Croatto, J. Severino. "The 'Nations' in the Salvific Oracles of Isaiah." *VT* 55/2 (2005): 143–61.

De Hoop, Raymond. "The Interpretation of Isaiah 56:1–9: Comfort or Criticism?" *JBL* 127/4 (2008): 671–95.
Douglas, Mary. "Responding to Ezra: The Priests and the Foreign Wives." *BibInt* 10/1 (2002): 1–23.
Finkelstein, Israel. "Archaeology and the List of Returnees in the Books of Ezra and Nehemiah." *PEQ* 140/1 (2008): 7–16.
———. "Jerusalem in the Persian (and Early Hellenistic) Period and the Wall of Nehemiah. *JSOT* 32/4 (2008): 501–20.
Frevel, Christian. *Mixed Marriages, Intermarriage, and Group Identity in the Second Temple Period.* New York: T&T Clark, 2011.
Fried, L. S. "The *'am ha'ares* in Ezra 4:4 and Persian Administration." Pages 123–45 in *Judah and the Judeans in the Persian Period.* Edited by O. Lipschits and M. Oeming. Winona Lake, Ind.: Eisenbrauns, 2006.
Grabbe, Lester L. "'They Shall Come Rejoicing to Zion'—Or Did They? The Settlement of Yehud in the Early Persian Period." Pages 116–27 in *Exile and Restoration Revisited: Essays on the Babylonian and Persian Periods in Memory of Peter R. Ackroyd.* Edited by G. N. Knoppers and L. L. Grabbe with D. Fulton. New York: T&T Clark, 2009.
———. "Triumph of the Pious or Failure of the Xenophobes? The Ezra-Nehemiah Reforms and Their Nachgeschichte." Pages 50–65 in *Jewish Local Patriotism and Self Identification,* Edited by S. Jones and S. Pearce. Sheffield: Sheffield Academic, 1998.
———. "Josephus and the Reconstruction of the Judean Restoration." *JBL* 106/2 (1987): 231–246.
Hammock, Clinton, "Isaiah 56:1–8 and the Redefining of the Restoration Judean Community." *BTB* 30/2 (2000): 46–57.
Ingrid Hjelm, "What Do Samaritans and Jews Have in Common? Recent Trends in Samaritan Studies." *CBR* 3/1 (2004): 9–59.
Janzen, David. *Witch-Hunts, Purity and Social Boundaries: The Expulsion of the Foreign Women in Ezra 9–10.* Sheffield: Sheffield Academic, 2002.
———. "Politics, Settlement, and Temple Community in Persian-Period Yehud." *CBQ* 64/3 (2002): 490–511.
Leuchter, Mark. "The Politics of Ritual Rhetoric: A Proposed Sociopolitical Context for the Redaction of Leviticus 1–16." *VT* 60/3 (2010): 345–65.
Olyan, Saul M. "Purity Ideology in Ezra-Nehemiah as a Tool to Reconstitute the Community." *JSOJ* 35/1 (2004): 1–16.
Sivertsev, Alexei. "Sects and Households: Social Structure of the Proto-Sectarian Movement of Nehemiah 10 and the Dead Sea Sect." *CBQ* 67/1 (2005): 59–78.
Smith-Christopher, D. L. "Between Ezra and Isaiah: Exclusion, Transformation, and Inclusion of the 'Foreigner' in Post-exilic Biblical Theology." Pages 117–42 in *Ethnicity and the Bible.* Edited by Mark G. Brett. Leiden: Brill, 1996.

Southwood, Katherine E. "'And They Could Not Understand Jewish Speech': Language, Ethnicity, and Nehemiah's Intermarriage Crisis." *JTS* 62/1 (2011): 1–19.

Talmon, S. "The Emergence of Jewish Sectarianism in the Early Second Temple Period." Pages 165–201 in *King, Cult and Calendar in Ancient Israel.* Edited by S. Talmon. Jerusalem: Magnes, 1986.

———. "The Internal Differentiation of Judaism within the Early Second Temple Period." Pages 16–43 in *Jewish Civilization in the Hellenistic Period.* Edited by S. Talmon. Sheffield: JSOT Press, 1991.

Washington, Harold C. "Israel's Holy Seed and the Foreign Women of Ezra-Nehemiah: A Kristevan Reading." *BibInt* 11/3 (2003): 427–37.

Zlotnick-Sivan, H. "The Silent Women of Yehud: Notes on Ezra 9–10." *JJS* 51/1 (2000): 3–18.

INTERNAL MIGRATIONS AND SOCIAL JUSTICE IN AMOS AND MICAH

Lin Yan

Much of the inspiration for this article comes from my own migration experience. I left my hometown Xinjiang Uygur when I was eighteen years old. Then, in succession I lived in other places in China: Chendu, Shanghai, and Hong Kong for three or four years; for nearly six years now I have been living in Shenzhen. Although I have never been outside of China until now, the experience of long-time sojourning in many places in China to me seems like residing overseas, because I had to face strange dialects, different customs, and new cultures wherever I went. This kind of living experience helps me understand deeply the meaning of the Chinese saying "Ten miles apart, but the customs are quite different." In fact, in China, many present provinces were treated as different countries during the Zhou Dynasty (BCE 1046–BCE 256), and a lot of Chinese people at that time traveled to other countries because of wars, trade, or something else, but in fact they were migrants and many of them lived in a state of diaspora.[1] In this sense, I treat myself as one who has migrated. In the light of such a migration experience, I see the prophets Amos and Micah as immigrants, too, because they left their hometowns and prophesied in big cities. My intention in this article is to review these two prophets' migration experience in the light of Chinese people's migration experience, and explore the possible relationship between these two prophets' migration identities and their passion for social justice.

THE BOOKS OF AMOS AND MICAH

In reviewing the book of Amos,[2] Robert B. Coote uses editorial criticism to analyze three stages of composition in the book. He points out stage A as the edition of Amos himself, which was composed roughly in the eighth century. Stage B is the edition of the Bethel editor, in the seventh century. Stage C is the work of the closing editor in the sixth century. Coote gives a theological explanation for every stage. The first half of his book is very helpful to my

---

[1] Liu Deng Han, *Chinese Literature: The Reconstruction of Crossing*. (Fuzhou: Fujian People's Publishing House, 2007), 35.

[2] Donoso S. Escobar makes a critical review on the social justice of the book of Amos, too, and I find it's very useful to my research. Donoso S. Escobar, "Social Justice in the Book of Amos," *RevExp*, 92 (1995): 173.

research.³ J. Albert Soggin's commentary uses philological/textual criticism. He translates the book of Amos, and then provides a historical and exegetical commentary for those who cannot read the original Hebrew.⁴ John D. W. Watts seems to study this book through form criticism and believes that there is the concept of eschatology in Amos's visions and oracles.⁵

In reviewing the book of Micah, Sung Hwa Chung suggests that Micah came from a rural area, but there is no obvious connection between Micah's rural identity and his passion for social justice in Sung's book.⁶ James Luther Mays uses form criticism and tries to understand prophecies in various settings.⁷ Juan I. Alfaro interprets the book of Micah in the context of liberation theology and applies this to the third-world reality.⁸

There are also some studies on the books of the prophets Amos and Micah within the context of the Eighth Century prophets: Henry McKeating notes that the Eighth Century prophets are different from earlier prophets whose words were not being written down at length.⁹ B. W. Anderson highlighted the distinctiveness of the "writing prophets" of Israel at the initial stage of their development and thought they were different from all known parallels in the ancient world.¹⁰ Hemchand Gossai distinguishes צדק and משפט which were used by the Eighth Century prophets and concludes both of these words were not only primarily terms of relationship but were used by the Eighth Century prophets against the many expressions of social injustice.¹¹

In this article, I will rely on the theory of Migration and Diaspora, which is often used in literary criticism, and inspect the possible relationship between Amos and Micah, these two prophets' migration identities, and their passions for social justice.

---

³ Robert B. Coote, *Amos among the Prophets: Composition and Theology* (Philadelphia: Fortress, 1981), 1–134.

⁴ J. Alberto.Soggin, *The Prophet Amos: A Translation and Commentary*, trans. John Bowden (London: SCM, 1987), 1–23.

⁵ John D. W. Watts, *Vision and Prophecy in Amos* (Macon, Ga.: Mercer University Press, 1997), 1–132.

⁶ Sung Hwa Chung, *The Rural Prophet: A Commentary on the Book of Micah* (Hong Kong: Christian Witness Press, 1957), 1–114.

⁷ James Luther Mays, *Micah: A Commentary* (London: SCM, 1976), 1–35.

⁸ Juan I. Alfaro, *Justice and Loyalty: A Commentary on the Book of Micah* (Grand Rapids: Eerdmans, 1989), 1–12.

⁹ Henry McKeating, *The Books of Amos, Hosea and Micah* (Cambridge: Cambridge University Press, 1971), 12–193.

¹⁰ Bernhard W. Anderson, *The Eighth Century Prophets: Amos, Hosea, Isaiah Micah*, (Philadelphia: Fortress, 1979), xiii–102.

¹¹ Hemchand Gossai, *Justice, Righteousness and the Social Critique of the Eighth-Century Prophets*, (New York: Peter Lang, 1993), 1–10.

INTERNATIONAL MIGRATION AND INTERNAL MIGRATION

The theme of Migration and Diaspora is widely discussed in the areas of cultural studies and literary criticism in mainland China. Generally speaking, such a theme has strong international characteristics. Migration often means people leave their countries and go to other countries, and I call such migration "international migration." As for Chinese migration, the Chinese leave China and go to other developed countries or foreign lands, which they hope can give them commercial and economic opportunities. When my myriad Chinese compatriots really become immigrants in western developed countries, they are brought into a social division of labor, which is highly peripheralized. Such a social division of labor nearly strips them of all their original possessions and identities, except for a lucky few.[12]

As mentioned above, I have never been overseas. However, I have the experience of living successively in many Chinese cities for several years, so I am able to be fully alive to the circumstances of my overseas compatriots. Like Chinese elites looking for chances overseas, numberless young people, including me, who have no opportunities to go abroad, gather in larger Chinese metropolises and hope to live a better life. Shenzhen where I currently live is one of the Chinese metropolises, and it is a typical Chinese migration city. By the end of 2010, there were 13.22 million permanent residents, of whom 2.51 million had *hukou* (household registration).[13] Most Shenzhen people who have *hukou* like me are not natives. Most impressively, Shenzhen is an empty city when the Chinese Lunar New Year approaches, because people are glad to return to their hometowns and celebrate this most important Chinese traditional festival with their relatives. These migrant workers are what I call "internal migrants," which is used in the broader sense of migration.

When I observe this local place of Shenzhen, I must ask myself: Do thousands of migrant workers in Shenzhen live better or more dignified lives than Chinese immigrants in San Francisco or Melbourne? These migrant workers in Shenzhen are economically disadvantaged, lack political interest, are sexually depressed and experience cultural aphasia. I think these living conditions of migrant workers are the result of the distribution of social resources and interests in China as a whole. Money centers in metropolises and workers flow to them. Chinese metropolises exploit, plunder, and colonize rural areas, not only economically, but also culturally.[14] In such a context, Chinese migrant

---

[12] Qian Chao Ying, *Diaspora Literature: The Local and the Oversea* (Shenzhen: Haitian Publishing House, 2007), 10.

[13] http://www.sz.gov.cn/cn/zjsz/szgl/201107/t20110712_1675680.htm

[14] Zhao He Mei, "Cultural Colonialism of the Urban to the Rural in Diaspora Literature of Mainland China: On Life by Lu Yao," *Journal of NUC (Social Sciences)*, 21(2005): 33–35.

workers are destined to experience a bitterness of fortune. For the same reason, Chinese migrations in western developed countries live in the same conditions with the migrant workers in Chinese metropolises because of international capital operation. Therefore, we witness similar diasporas by those who sojourn in alien lands, whether or not it is called "overseas."

As we know it, Amos came from Tekoa, a small village near the desert region of Judah, and prophesied in Samaria, the capital of the northern kingdom. The prophet Micah came from Moresheth, a small town, and prophesied in Jerusalem, the capital of the southern kingdom. In my opinion, the prophets Amos and Micah belong to internal migrations, and this identity (internal migration) has a relationship to their passions for social justice.[15]

MIGRATION IN BOTH SPACE AND TIME

We have divided migration into internal migration and international migration, and found there is no strict border between native countries and overseas when understanding migration in the perspective of space. In fact, migration also can be understood in the perspective of time.

Not all people are aware that the whole of modern life often begins with some form of cultural diaspora, population movement, and fatal suspension of the familiar landscape. Modern people consciously or forcibly remove themselves or are removed from their primary contacts, such as families, lands, and ethics, and go into a state of rootlessness and wandering. Many people have experienced this. The Western world is like this, not to mention the Third World, which is forced to change by the Western world. Of course, the former is active, systematic, and organic, and the latter is root rupturing, structure breaking, and disintegrates the culture.[16] Take China for example, which has been experiencing great changes since 1840 because of the effects of events such as the two opium Wars (1840–1842, 1856–1860), the Taiping rebellion (1851–1864), the Sino-Japanese War (1894–1895), the Wu Hsu Reform (1898), the Revolution of 1911, the May Fourth Movement (1919), the War of Resistance against Japan (1937–1945), the establishment of the People's Republic of China (1949), the Great Proletarian Cultural Revolution (1966–1976), and most recently, the Reform and Opening-Up (1976–).

Chinese people have been coded from system to fashion and from thinking to language for more than 150 years but the result is likely to be an uncomfortable miscoding. Few people like the Chinese have experienced several fundamental catastrophes of social ecology and cultural spirit within the time

---

[15] Strictly speaking, Amos is an international migrant considering the fact that the northern kingdom was separated from the southern kingdom, but I regard Amos as an internal migrant too.

[16] Qian Chao Ying, *Diaspora Literature*, 9.

span of one generation. Chinese history has increasingly become a kind of abstract consciousness, instead of a concrete foundation for life and a spiritual source. The past could not save the Chinese, but we haven't created our modern history. How can we overcome this kind of rootless anxiety? There are many novels such as Ba Jin's *Home*, narrating family quarrels, revolting against one's parents, and difficulties outside the home, in the history of modern Chinese literature. Such stories should be read as the symbol of our cultural diaspora and spiritual migration.[17]

In my opinion, migration can also be understood in the dimension of time, especially with reference to cultural rupturing and spiritual drifting, caused by social changes. In such situations, people compare the present with the past. Many Shenzhen literary works talk about memories and re-visiting the inland, such as *A City of 26 Questions and Answers* and *We Are Not the Same Kind of Human*.[18] In these novels, internal migrants' primary contacts seem to be their lost paradise (or hell), and they know Shenzhen by comparing the inland.[19]

The prophets Amos and Micah's ages are not too far away from the time of the establishment of the Israelite monarchy, which was a very important event in the history of Israel. Then, the division of the united kingdom was the great change in Israelite society. Subsequently, the northern kingdom was destroyed. The Israelites, including the prophets Amos and Micah (the northern kingdom still existed when Amos prophesied), experienced cultural diaspora and spiritual migration in less than three hundred years. They also talk about and recall Jacob, the Exodus, and the divided kingdom referring to these old matters and traditions. So, Amos and Micah are what I call real migrants, not only in space, but also in time.

INTERNAL MIGRATION IDENTITIES AND PASSION FOR SOCIAL JUSTICE

In this part I will analyze the possible relationship between Amos and Micah's identities as internal migrants and their passion for social justice through a close reading. The discussion will be based on the following four aspects:

Humble Prophets and Noble Cities

Amos and Micah were two prophets who came from small places in the Book of Prophets. Amos came from Tekoa, a small village near Jerusalem (1:1). He was a herdsman and a dresser of sycamore tress (7:14). He came to Samaria, the capital of Israel and prophesied there, but was expelled by Amaziah, the priest of Bethel (7:10–17). Micah came from Moresheth (1:1), also a small town halfway

---

[17] Qian Chao Ying, *Diaspora Literature*, 9.

[18] Wang Xiao Ni, *A City of 26 Questions and Answers*. Special Zone Literature, 5 (2004), 4–83; Wu Jun, *We Are Not the Same Kind of Human* (Beijing: Writers Publishing House, 2004), 1–147.

[19] Qian Chao Ying, *Diaspora Literature*, 9.

between Jerusalem and the seacoast, and he prophesied in Jerusalem, the capital of Judah. Amos and Micah had arisen from humble origins, and these two humble prophets prophesied in noble cities. [20]

When Amos and Micah went to Samaria and Jerusalem respectively, they were shocked by sights they had never seen. We find clues to what they saw and experienced in their proclamations: "The people of Israel who live in Samaria...with the corner of a couch and part of a bed" (Amos 3:12);[21] "The winter house as well as the summer house...the house of ivory...the great house" (Amos 3:15); "Cows of Bashan who are on Mount Samaria"(Amos 4:1); "Beds of ivory," "Eat lambs from the flock and calves from the stall," "Who sing idle songs to the sound of the harp...who drink wine from bowls, and anoint themselves with the finest oils" (Amos 6:4–6); "Your wealthy are full of violence" (Mic 6:12). In eighth century Israel and Judah, the ruling elite were the governing class, and they controlled the greater amount of wealth in the society and exercised dominion over the peasantry. They controlled most of the land, although the large majority of these elite lived in cities, especially the capital. Money centered in big cities, and sins and injustices afflicted these noble places.[22]

Amos and Micah were extremely angry with what they saw and this anger is evidenced in their proclamations: "They sell the righteous for silver and the needy for a pair of sandals; they who trample the head of the poor into the dust of the earth, and push the afflicted out of the way; father and son go in to the same girl...they lay themselves down beside every altar on garments taken in pledge; and in the house of their God they drink wine bought with fines they imposed" (Amos 2:6–8); "Who oppress the poor, who crush the needy" (Amos 4: 2); "You that turn justice to wormwood, and bring righteousness to the ground!" (Amos 5:7); "You trample on the poor and take from them levies of grain...you who afflict the righteous, who take a bribe, and push aside the needy in the gate" (Amos 5:12); "You have turned justice into poison and the fruit of righteousness into wormwood" (Amos 6:12); "We will make the ephah small and the shekel great, and practice deceit with false balances, buying the poor for silver and the needy for a pair of sandals, and selling the sweepings of the wheat" (Amos 8:5–6); "They covet fields, and seize them; houses, and take them away; they oppress householder and house, people and their inheritance" (Mic 2:2); "You rise up against my people as an enemy; you strip the robe from the peaceful, from those who pass by trustingly with no thought of war. The women of my people you drive out from their pleasant houses; from their young children you take away my glory forever" (Mic 2:8–9); "You who hate the good and love the evil, who

---

[20] Juan I. Alfaro, *Justice and Loyalty: A Commentary on the Book of Micah*, 14.

[21] The biblical texts cited in this article come from the NRSV.

[22] Robert B. Coote, *Amos among the Prophets: Composition and Theology*, 25.

tear the skin off my people, and the flesh off their bones, who eat the flesh of my people, flay their skin off them, break their bones in pieces, and chop them up like meat in a kettle, like flesh in a caldron" (Mic 3:2–4); "Its rulers give judgment for a bribe, its priests teach for a price, its prophets give oracles for money" (Mic 3:11); "Your wealthy are full of violence" (Mic 6:12). Most of their prophecies focus on social justice, and condemn the rich who oppress the needy.

In fact, other prophets namely, Isaiah, Jeremiah, Ezekiel, Hosea, Nahum, Habakkuk, Zephaniah, Haggai, Zechariah, and Malachi also speak of and address issues of social justice.[23] However, different backgrounds produce different interests. For example, Isaiah, a man of the city and an adviser to the royal court, could not go so far as to predict the destruction of the temple, which Yahweh had chosen as his "dwelling place."[24] Amos and Micah had humble origins, and they sojourned in the capitals, centers of the evils caused by international and internal trade and prophesied as internal immigrants.[25] Amos and Micah raged as men of God against wickedness, and their anger was mixed with a rural man's disgust at urban civilization.[26]

Recalling the Past and Revisiting Old Places

Recalling the past and revisiting old places are deeply involved in the prophecies of Amos and Micah. If we comb these prophecies, we will find that they recalled the ancestors of Israel and some significant places of that time: "You will show faithfulness to Jacob and unswerving loyalty to Abraham, you have sworn to our ancestors from the days of old" (Mic 7:20). "I abhor the pride of Jacob and hate his strongholds" (Amos 6: 8); "I overthrew some of you, as when God overthrew Sodom and Gomorrah (Amos 4:11)"; "All this is for the transgression of Jacob" (Mic 1:5); "Should this be said, O house of Jacob? Is the LORD's patience exhausted?"(Mic 2:7); "I will surely gather all of you, O Jacob" (Mic 2:12); "Listen, you heads of Jacob and rulers of the house of Israel!"(Mic 3:1; 3:9); "To declare to Jacob his transgression and to Israel his sin" (Mic 3:8); "but are not grieved over the ruin of Joseph!" (Amos 6:6); "The God of hosts will be gracious to the remnant of Joseph." The prophets' criticism of Jacob here seems to suggest that God's people in the eighth century were just like Jacob who still did not receive God's blessing.

We also find many references to the Exodus and the wilderness traditions: "I brought you up out of the land of Egypt, and led you forty years in the wilderness, to possess the land of the Amorite" (Amos 2:10); "O people of Israel, against the

---

[23] Hemchand Gossai, *Justice, Righteousness and the Social Critique of the Eighth-Century Prophets*, 152–66.
[24] Anderson, *The Eighth Century Prophets*, 41.
[25] William Sanford LaSor, David Allan Hubbard and Frederic Wm. Bush, *Old Testament Survey: The Message, Form, and Background of the Old Testament*, 2nd ed.; Grand Rapids: Eerdmans, 1996), 245.
[26] Henry McKeating, *The Books of Amos, Hosea and Micah*, 31.

whole family that I brought up out of the land of Egypt" (Amos 3:1); "Did you bring to me sacrifices and offerings the forty years in the wilderness, O house of Israel?" (Amos 5:25); "Did I not bring Israel up from the land of Egypt" (Amos 9:7) "For I brought you up from the land of Egypt, and redeemed you from the house of slavery; and I sent before you Moses, Aaron, and Miriam ... you may know the saving acts of the LORD." (Mic 6:4–5); "As in the days when you came out of the land of Egypt, show us marvelous things" (Mic 7:15). The Exodus and the wilderness traveling were great events that embodied God's salvation. The prophets hoped that the people would repent and establish a good relationship with God as before.

Reference is also made to the kings and the places of the northern kingdom: "For you have kept the statutes of Omri and all the works of the house of Ahab, and you have followed their counsels." (Mic 6:16) "Let them feed in Bashan and Gilead as in the days of old" (Mic 7: 14). When Micah was an old man, the northern kingdom was ruined. Micah warned Judah and gave them hope.

Israel as a nation had experienced many great changes in the eighth century: Israel as a nation experienced a cultural rupturing and spiritual drifting brought on by social changes. In such a situation the prophets used to compare the present with the past: using Jacob who didn't receive God's blessing provided an analogy for the Israelites in their time. They recalled the salvation of the Mosaic time in order to encourage the Israelites to repent and to stress God's sustained love. They did this while recalling and revisiting symbols while in a state of cultural diaspora and spiritual migration. In the prophets' view, all the injustice and unrighteousness of their time was caused by the rejection of divine sovereignty, the Mosaic covenant tradition, and the consequent social changes. I think it is the reason that prophets repeatedly recall the past and revisit old places.

Righteousness and Justice

When we read these two books, we can often find righteousness (צדק) and justice (משפט) are used as a word pair (Amos 2:6; 3:10; 5:7; 5:12; 5:15; 5:24; 6:12; Mic 3:1; 3:9; 6:8). What are the differences between them? Some opinions of scholars in the field might help us understand the many nuances of these two very significant terms. Hemchand Gossai in his discussion of these terms suggests that the fundamental factor in many expressions of injustice in the eighth century is the corruption of Israel's cult. The cult epitomizes Israel's relationship with Yahweh, and a corrupted cult means a broken relationship between Israel and Yahweh, leading to injustice in society. So, the emphasis on righteousness and justice indicates the prophets' interest in the restoration of the people's broken relationship with Yahweh (righteousness) and with each other (justice).²⁷ Jannie du Preez points out that justice is associated with the protection of the weak and the poor, and righteousness belongs to those who fulfill the responsibilities to others (for example, Tamar [Gen 38] is deemed righteous because she does her best to bear a child for her dead husband).²⁸ Fred Guyette considers that the concept of justice in the biblical tradition is broad and "thick," and it often expresses the basic relationship between God and his people and depended on story, imagery, and metaphor (such as the basket of summer fruit, the crooked scales and the plumb line).²⁹ Martha Moore-Keish distinguishes God's justice and human justice, and believes human justice expresses God's justice, too. Moore-Keish also believes that justice should be understood through true sacrifice.³⁰ With the help of these studies, we are able to distinguish between the use of righteousness and justice in the books of Amos and Micah. Together they constitute the relationship with God and the poor. Injustice and unrighteousness include breach in the relationship with God and the oppression of the poor, because God is the protector of the poor, and oppressing the poor means offending God.

Alfaro identifies four groups of powerful persons that were responsible for social justice in the book of Micah: "(1) Political powers: princes, elders, military officials who exploited the people and used their power to steal and abuse; (2) Judicial powers: judges, elders who had made justice a convenient commodity for their enrichment; (3) Religious powers: priests and prophets whose real god was money; (4) Economic powers: the rich, landowners, hoarders and merchants."³¹ These ruling elites were severely criticized by Amos and Micah who belonged to those of humble origins.

From Where Did the Prophets Derive Their Authority?

Amos and Micah who had humble origins prophesied in the noble cities. But I wonder who would believe in what these outsiders said? When Amos prophesied in Samaria, he was driven out by Amaziah the priest of Bethel (Amos 7:10). So, we have reasons to believe these two prophets did not have the approval of the people of that time. As a prophet, he who could receive God's revelation is indispensible, and it is an effectual standard to distinguish true prophets and false prophets. Amos and Micah were true prophets, and they declared in the full

---

²⁷ Hemchand Gossai, *Justice, Righteousness and the Social Critique of the Eighth–Century Prophets*, 310–11.
²⁸ Jannie du Preez, "'Let Justice Roll on Like…': Some Explanatory Notes on Amos 5: 24," *JTSA*,109 (2001): 96.
²⁹ Fred Guyette, "Amos the Prophet: A Meditation on the Richness of 'Justice,'" *JBQ* 36 (2008): 19.
³⁰ Martha Moore-Keish, "'Do Justice': Micah 6:8," *Journal for Preachers*, 5 (2010): 20–25.
³¹ Juan I. Alfaro, *Justice and Loyalty: A Commentary on the Book of Micah*, 7–8.

power of the Spirit of God and on the side of divine justice (Mic 3: 8; Amos 3: 7–8).[32] On the contrary, false prophets gave oracles for money, and they served the rich and the ruling elite. So, although Amos and Micah had humble origins, they were full of the power of the Spirit of God, and their authority as prophets came from God. Amos and Micah continue the prophetic tradition that begins with Moses and then inherited by Elijah, Elisha and many other prophets.

CONCLUSION

In this article, migration involves both space and time. In terms of space, migration can be divided into internal migration and international migration. This article uses internal migration to refer to those who sojourn in a place other than their hometown but still within their country. Migration can also be understood in the perspective of time as cultural and spiritual rupturing giving rise to an experience of diaspora, which is common to people of this time and age. In this broad sense, this article holds that Amos and Micah, from humble origins, are internal migrants who prophesied in noble cities. They also experienced the Israelites' spiritual Diaspora, and they recalled the past and made mention of significant sites that functioned as symbols of cultural diaspora and spiritual migration. All injustice and unrighteousness of the prophets' time was caused by the rejection of divine sovereignty and that of the Mosaic covenant tradition and resulted in huge social changes. This writer believes Amos and Micah's migration identities have a relationship to their passion for social justice. Furthermore, this article suggests that Amos and Micah cared about social justice because of their humble origins. Although Amos and Micah had humble origins, they were full of the power of the Spirit of God, and their authority as prophets came from God. Admittedly, what we have observed in this study is far from complete and it requires further research, especially the relationship of the prophets' migration identities in the perspective of time and their passion for social justice.

We are all strangers and foreigners on the earth (Heb 11:13), no matter whether we are migrants or not. The prophets Amos and Micah are representative of internal migration, but they convey a kind of universal value. Thus, migration and diaspora also should be read in the context of the whole people's fate.

---

[32] M. Daniel Carroll R., "A Passion for Justice and the Conflicted Self: Lessons from the Book of Micah," *Journal of Psychology and Christianity*, 25 (2006): 174.

BIBLIOGRAPHY

Alberto, Soggin J. *The Prophet Amos: A Translation and Commentary.* Trans. John Bowden, London: SCM, 1987.

Alfero, Juan I. *Justice and Loyalty: A Commentary on the Book of Micah.* Grand Rapids: Eerdmans, 1989.

Anderson, Bernhard W. *The Eighth Century Prophets: Amos, Hosea, Isaiah. Micah*, Philadelphia: Fortress, 1979.

Carroll, Mark Daniel. 1979. *Contexts for Amos's Prophetic Poetics in Latin American Perspective.* Sheffield: JSOT Press, 1979.

Carroll, R., M. Daniel. "A Passion for Justice and the Conflicted Self: Lessons from the Book of Micah." *Journal of Psychology and Christianity* 25 (2006): 169–76.

Coote, B. Robert. *Amos among the Prophets: Composition and Theology.* Philadelphia: Fortress, 1981.

Doorly, William J. *Prophet of Justice: Understanding the Book of Amos.* New York: Paulist, 1989.

Escobar, Donoso S. "Social Justice in the Book of Amos." *RevExp* 92 (1995): 169–74.

Gossai, Hemchand. *Justice, Righteousness and the Social Critique of the Eighth-Century Prophets.* New York: Peter Lang, 1993.

Guyette, Fred. "Amos the Prophet: A Meditation on the Richness of 'Justice.'" *JBQ* 36 (2008): 15–21.

Hayes, John H. *Amos the Eighth-Century Prophet: His Time and His Preaching.* Nashville, Tenn.: Abingdon, 1988.

Kelley, Page H. *Amos: Prophet of Social Justice.* Grand Rapids: Baker, 1972.

LaSor, William Sanford, David Allan Hubbard and Frederic Wm. Bush. *Old Testament Survey: The Message, Form, and Background of the Old Testament.* 2nd ed. Grand Rapids: Eerdmans, 1996.

Liu, Deng Han *Chinese Literature: The Reconstruction of Crossing.* Fuzhou: Fujian People's Publishing House, 2007.

Mays, James Luther. *Micah: A Commentary.* London: SCM, 1976.

McKeating, Henry. *The Books of Amos, Hosea and Micah.* Cambridge: Cambridge University Press, 1971.

Preez, Jannie du. "'Let Justice Roll on Like…' Some Explanatory Notes on Amos 5:24." *JTSA* 109, (2001): 95–98.

Qian, Chao Ying. *Diaspora Literature: The Local and the Oversea.* Shenzhen: Haitian Publishing House, 2007.

Sung, Hwa Chung. *The Rural Prophet: A Commentary on the Book of Micah.* Hong Kong: Christian Witness, 1957.

Wang, Xiao Ni. *A City of 26 Questions and Answers.* Special Zone Literature 5 (2004): 4–83.

Watts, John D. W. *Vision and Prophecy in Amos.* Macon, Ga.: Mercer University Press, 1997.

Wu, Jun. *We Are Not the Same Kind of Human.* Beijing: Writers Publishing House, 2004.
Zhao, He Mei. "Cultural Colonialism of the Urban to the Rural in Diaspora Literature of Mainland China: On Life by Lu Yao." *Journal of NUC (Social Sciences)* 21 (2005): 33–35.

DESIRING THE EMPIRE: READING THE BOOK OF ESTHER IN TWENTY-FIRST CENTURY KOREA

Yani Yoo

Globalization seems to have made global citizens want more materials than ever. As I live in twenty-first century Korea, which has gone through big changes in a short time, I see that Koreans are not exempt from desiring more material things and live constantly under the pressure of being judged by how much they have. In several decades Korea has grown from a country receiving financial aid from other countries to a country giving aid to others. They call it the miracle of the Han River. Korea is also a member of the Organization for Economic Cooperation and Development (OECD) nations and receives migrant labor from other countries. But the world financial crisis of 2008 resulted in a substantial percentage of irregular workers in Korea. Corporate companies try to make more money by hiring people on a part-time basis or on a contract basis. Migrant workers in Korea are paid much less than Koreans and are not given a chance to apply for the green card. Everyone is in the money game and desires a better life, especially in the material sense.

Reading the book of Esther in twenty-first century Korea gives me a different perspective. This essay is an attempt to read the book as a story of human desires, wanting materials, power, and sex.[1] The narrator projects his desires through the character of Mordecai. The narrator supports, praises, envies, and wants the power, material abundance, and sex that are available to the emperor, the representative symbol of the empire. The narrator's desires are disguised within the survival of oppressed minorities and are hidden behind his skillful literary plot and devices. Just as the book of Lamentations depicts human loss and sorrow, and the Song of Songs praises human carnal love, the book of Esther in my opinion frankly describes human desire of material things, power, and sex.

The king does not seem to care about conflicts among minority groups exemplified by the conflict between Mordecai the Jew and Haman the Agagite. The king also avoids their united rebellion against the empire. The emperor neither risks nor loses anything. This kind of literature teaches the powerful how to handle minorities and thus is a dangerous story. It is our contention that the book of Esther after all is an empire story promoting its interests, rather than a survival story of the Diaspora.

---

[1] Carol M. Bechtel mentions something similar in passing. She says that when this story is read in the first world where the reader is used to aspiring to the lifestyle of the rich and famous the reader praises the success of the king and secretly wants his palace and possessions. *Esther*. Interpretation (Louisville: Westminster John Knox, 2011; Korean translation, Korean Presbyterian Publishing, 2010), 58.

In the first part we will try to understand the story and characters differently from other scholars and to uncover the narrator's hidden motives and desires. In the second part we will relate our reading of the book of Esther to the Korean dealings with migrant workers in the present time. Korea used to be a country comprised of a single ethnic group but now is multicultural. The country faces many new issues related to the multicultural changes taking place today. It is against this background that the essay will see what implications the reading of the book as a human desire story and an empire story would leave for Korean readers.

THE DIASPORA REALITY IN THE BOOK OF ESTHER:

WHAT IS SO TOUGH ABOUT IT?

Many scholars have argued that the book of Esther shows how the Diaspora successfully survived within the tough reality of a discriminatory Persian empire. Scholars use words such as "anxious," "precarious," and "vulnerable" to depict the reality of the Diaspora. Does the book really describe the tough reality of the Diaspora? Edward Greenstein assumed that Esther's portrait of life in the Diaspora reflects the situation of its Diaspora audience:

> The scroll's representation of Jewish life in the Diaspora is fraught with anxiety. . . Living in such a precarious position, vulnerable to the suspicion and enmity of the majority population, a people would need at some time to give vent to its repressed tensions. Purim fills this need, as does the Esther scroll.[2]

Most scholars seem to read the book this way. According to Frederick Bush, the narrator of the book describes the Diaspora world as a dangerous and uncertain place.[3] Sidnie Ann White goes a step further and says that although Esther's use of sex is questionable, it is understandable because it was the only means available to women under patriarchy and in the tough exilic life.[4] Even if the reality was tough, immoral means to achieve a goal cannot be rationalized.

---

[2] Edward Greenstein, "A Jewish Reading of Esther," in *Judaic Perspectives on Ancient Israel*, ed. Jacob Neusner, et al. (Philadelphia: Fortress, 1987), 235.

[3] Frederic Bush, *Ruth, Esther*, WBC 9 (Nashville, Tenn.: Thomas Nelson, 1996; Korean translation, Solomon, Seoul: 2007), 491.

[4] Naomi Harris Rosenblatt, "Esther and Samson," *BRev* 15:1 (1999): 22; Sidnie Ann White, "Esther: A Feminine Model for Jewish Diaspora," in *Gender and Difference in Ancient Israel*, ed. P. L. Day (Minneapolis, Minn.: Fortress, 1989), 161–77. I find this comment questionable. We do not have to promote the idea that using feminine charm for success is acceptable or even recommendable in the name of women's tough

Elsie Stern observes the book differently and points out that the Jewishness of the Jewish characters does not affect their status, their access to power, their actions, or their worldview.[5] Mordecai's access to the area "in front of the harem courtyard" (2.11) as well as his fortuitous presence "in the royal gate" (2.21) suggest that he is a royal courtier or at least a minor player in court politics. The king's willingness to dress him in the trappings of royalty and Mordecai's rapid rise to second in command at the end of the book further demonstrate that his Jewishness is no obstacle to political favor and power in Susa. Similarly, after Esther reveals her identity to the king, he does not make any commotion about her or Jews in general. Rather, he continues to treat her positively. Nor do the residents of Susa. In fact, when Haman's decree of destruction goes out, the city of Susa is dismayed (3.15). When Mordecai leaves the presence of the king in the royal apparel, the city of Susa rejoices (8.15). In short, Persia, the emperor, and the Susa citizens do not show systematic discrimination against Jews or other ethnic groups. This kind of country and people are hard to find even in the twenty-first century world!

The narrator's presenting the story as a crisis caused by the Jewishness of main characters can mislead the reader. When the reader focuses on the crisis and its resolution and on the literary plot and devices, the reader can be lost. Maybe the narrator does not tell the whole story. Or perhaps, it is the reader's job to find out the narrator's hidden intentions and desires. When we read the story as a conflict story between the weak Diaspora and the powerful locals, as a conflict story between a beautiful Diaspora heroine and a vicious male high official, the interests of the empire and the desires of the narrator will remain invisible to the reader.

DESIRING THE EMPIRE

Desiring Power, Food, and Sex

Scholars have observed that exaggeration is a major trait in the book of Esther. Descriptions about power, feast, and sex are overly stated. Violence can be understood in the same way. But it goes together with power. In our interpretation, exaggeration is not a simple literary device, but a code that reveals the desires of the narrator. The desires for power, food, and sex are blatantly expressed in the first two chapters of the book and set the tone for the whole book. Chapter one contains three feasts and each emphasizes one desire.

---

reality. A recent study also finds it ineffective in the long run. Cf. http://blog.joins.com/yiyoyong/

[5] Stern concludes that the book of Esther is a story that the Jews living in Palestine ridicule the Jews living in the Diaspora. Elsie R. Stern, "Esther and the Politics of Diaspora," *JQR* 100.1 (Winter 2010): 25–53.

The first feast for the officials and ministers focuses on displaying the power and majesty of the emperor. The second one for the people of Susa focuses on the luxury of the palace, abundance in food, and the culture of high society. The third feast focuses on women, especially the (un)availability of sex. In the rest of the book, feasts are in the center of the plot. Esther invites key players of the power game, the king and Haman, to her feasts to meet her goal. Feasts offer her good excuses to invite the king despite the protocol of not showing up before him without permission. Feasts become the site of creation and resolution of crises.

Power

The power that the narrator desires is both political and material. The narrator reports that Ahasuerus ruled over 127 provinces from India to Ethiopia. The narrator exaggerates the number of provinces since Persia had only twenty provinces. In the third year of his reign Ahasuerus hosted a banquet for his officials and ministers. The narrator repeats the list of the invitees: they are the army of Persia and Media and the nobles and governors of the provinces. The banquet lasted 180 days. The narrator notes that the occasion displayed the great wealth of his kingdom and the splendor and pomp of the majesty of the king. The narrator emphasizes the aspect of power through the first feast.

After this feast, the second feast is offered to the Susa citizens. There was even a women's feast hosted by Queen Vashti. In describing this feast alone, the narrator makes mention of the luxurious decorations of the palace. So the narrator takes the viewpoint of a man from Susa, a commoner sitting in the banquet, looking around at the decorations, and being overwhelmed by them. He raises his head, looks around, and sees that there are white cotton curtains and blue hangings tied with cords of fine linen and purple to silver rings and marble pillars (1:6). While the feast is held in the courtyard, he notices curtains and cords of linen, materials often used indoors. If they belonged to the indoors, we wonder if he peeked into the inside of the palace building. There are also couches of gold and silver on a mosaic pavement of porphyry, marble, and mother-of-pearl, and colored stones (1:6). Then he takes a look at his goblet. The goblets are golden and these are also of different kinds. This Susa commoner is deeply impressed by the luxury of the palace.

Only for this feast does the narrator also mention the quantity of food, especially the wine. "The royal wine was lavished according to the bounty of the king. Drinking was by flagons, without restraint" (1:7–8). There is another element that the narrator adds to the description of this feast. It is culture. "And drinking was according to the law, no one was compelled. For the king had given orders to all the officials of his palace to do as each one desired," (1:8). The reader suspects if this refers to a different culture, a culture of high society. Maybe, then, commoners are compelled to drink. The Susa man is overwhelmed by the noble culture of the palace and the upper class. The reader also wonders if the narrator is here revealing his envies. Detailed descriptions of the imperial splendor and material abundance reflect the narrator's aspirations. He wants what the emperor has.

Food

The book is about sumptuous food and feasts. The book contains the word "feast" more than any other book in the Bible. There are ten feasts in the book and in chapter 1 alone there are three.[6] The first one for the officials and ministers lasts for 180 days. The second feast for the Susaites lasts for seven days. The last one is Queen Vashti's and it is for women. All these feasts point to abundant food. Scholars often consider the long duration of the feasts as mere exaggeration or exaggeration with mockery.[7]

The abundance of food is also expressed through abundance of wine. It is twice emphasized: "The royal wine was lavished according to the bounty of the king. Drinking was by flagons, without restraint," (1:7). Feast after feast, the duration of 180 days and seven days, and even a feast among women only— all emphasize abundance in food and material.

Sex

Right after reporting the existence of a women's feast, the narrator states the king's sexual interest. The king wants to show off his beautiful queen to the people and the officials. But she refuses to follow the king's command. What interests us is that the king sends not one eunuch, but seven to bring Vashti before the king. The king seems to know already that it would be hard to make her come. The reader wonders if Vashti's refusal reflects the narrator's lack of confidence about women.

The king gets angry and consults with the law experts. The king ends up following the advice of an expert and issues a decree, declaring that every man should be master in his own house.

Aspiration of the empire requires having the emperor's woman.[8] There should be seven eunuchs, or more. They do not form any rivalry. Eunuchs in chapter one and other chapters seem to function in the same manner. They are safe helpers who can support the aspirations of the narrator. But in Vashti's case the potential voyeurism fails because of her refusal.

Out of three representative elements of the empire, namely, power, food, and sex, food appears easily, power is to be grabbed in the process of struggle, and sex seems the hardest to get. Sex here refers to women, as the story takes a

---

[6] Ten separate events are described using the root *shth*: nine events with the noun *mishteh*, and one with the verb *shatah*.

[7] Bush, *Ruth, Esther*, 492.

[8] Absalom took David's concubines and David took Nabal's wife, Abigail. It symbolizes complete subjugation of the competitor.

male viewpoint. Vashti's refusal implies that having the emperor's woman and thus having the empire wholly is not easy. Then, the woman must be punished and revenged. That is why Vashti is made to vanish.

Chapter 2 seems to be devoted to the expression of the narrator's sexual desire through a beauty contest and selection of a new queen. Selecting a new queen through a contest is another form of voyeurism. Hegai, a eunuch, takes care of the beautiful candidates. The narrator appreciates them through the safe eyes of the eunuch. It is therefore no wonder that the eunuch is positively described. The only standards expected of the future queen are beauty and skill in sex. According to Bush, this is a satire and it casts cynical and prejudicial views on the Persian king and his palace.[9] But we can read it as an explicit expression of desires. For the narrator, beauty and her sex seem to matter the most. That is why the expression, "the girl to go in to the king" appears five times stressing the role of the beauties (2:12–15). Intriguingly, the narrator takes a male viewpoint in describing a woman to have sex with the king, a man. Outside the book, the phrase, "to go into" is used to describe the act of a man having sex with a woman. The narrator seems to be demasculinizing the king and actually dominates him. The beauties seem to be men on the inside. At least, one of them will act like a man later. So chapter 2 sets the tone for the rest of the story in terms of gender politics.

It is interesting to note that after Esther was taken into the king's palace, Mordecai will never see her again or talk to her face to face in the rest of the book. The narrator's aspiration is expressed through Mordecai. When Esther becomes the king's woman she will not be available to a commoner. What Mordecai could do was to walk around in front of the court of the harem every day (2:11). Even the "conversation" between Mordecai and Esther that involves the famous expression, "If I perish, I perish," happens indirectly through Hathach, a eunuch (4:16).

The three elements, food, power, and sex are closely intertwined and if access to any one of these is missing, it disqualifies a person to be truly powerful.

CHARACTERS: ALL GREEDY AND EVIL

To expose the hidden desires and motives in the book we also need to scrutinize characterization. Although major characters play different roles and show different personalities, they can also represent the many aspects and desires of the narrator. In understanding characters in literature, Linda Day points out that as readers, we analyze characters as if they were alive.[10] We view characters

---

[9] Bush, *Ruth, Esther*, 493.

[10] Linda Day, *Three Faces of a Queen: Characterization in the Book of Esther*, JSOTSup 186 (Sheffield: Sheffield Academic, 1995), 20–21.

from our own individual experiences and our own situations in real life. So interpreting a character, just as interpreting a text, is a subjective activity.

The narrator employs literary strategies via characterization and rich literary plot and devices. The reader is trapped in them. So the reader follows the destiny of the main figures, namely Esther and Mordecai, and takes part in their crisis, overcomes it with them, and rejoices in their victory. In the meantime, the reader misses what the narrator silences and promotes behind the scene. Further, a scholars' dominant understanding of characters may also hinder the reader to see them in their own life situations. The reader is entitled to encounter characters in their own way.

King Ahasuerus

Adele Berlin sees major characters of the book as types, as farce uses exaggerated or caricatured character types.[11] So Ahasuerus is "a caricature of a pampered and bumbling monarch, a ruler ruled by his advisor."[12] Scholars think that the king is depicted as obsessed with honor, acting capriciously, arrogant, and showing off.[13] For example, the king hears his servants' suggestions on important matters and follows them. He offers half the kingdom to Esther several times (5:3, 8; 7:2) and his signet ring to Haman and Mordecai (3:10, 12; 8:2, 8, 10). Scholars see this as his taking his kingship lightly. But seeing the king as a mindless buffoon can mislead the reader.

Carol M. Bechtel adds another dimension to this understanding of the king: the king is a buffoon but is dangerous.[14] We take a step further and argue that the king is more dangerous than anyone in the story. Power and danger go together. A powerful emperor is unthinkable without being dangerous. Esther is tellingly afraid of accessing him, although it involves the king's permission. So the aspects of the king that scholars understood as stupid or clown-like can be seen as his proud freedom that a powerful king can enjoy.

The king is not an uncontrollable drunkard or a fool. Rather, he is a leader who bestows respect and freedom on his citizens. The king's moderation is shown in the second feast: "And drinking was according to the law, no one was compelled. For the king had given orders to all the officials of his palace to do as each one desired." (1:8). He does not let his servants rule the kingdom, either. When he hears his servants' suggestions and follows them it does not necessarily mean that he does not have his own mind. He can be seen as utilizing a consultation system. We can say that the king just likes the suggestion of the law expert and he issues a decree that a husband's voice be heard at home

---

[11] Adele Berlin, xix; B. W. Jones, , et. al.
[12] Berlin, *Esther: The Traditional Hebrew Text with the New JPS Translation* (Philadelphia: Jewish Publication Society, 2001), xx.
[13] Bush, *Ruth, Esther*, 492.
[14] Bechtel, *Esther*, 59.

(1:22). He also likes the suggestion of his servants that pretty virgins be sought (2:4). Listening to Haman, the king issues a decree that allows for the elimination of the Jews (chap. 3). When Esther's appeal sounds good he chooses it, although it contradicts his previous decision. These activities of the king can be understood as his exercising power. He just makes a decision that serves his best interest in a given time. That is what a powerful king does. The decrees are to be unchangeable and that indicates his absolute power. After all, the irrevocable decree to destroy the Jews was revoked later and the new decree to support the Jews is described as irrevocable (8:8). The emperor had that much power to do it. His offering of half the kingdom or his royal ring to others does not necessarily mean that he is not a serious ruler. He is so powerful and rich that he can carelessly throw words. He can also afford to be proud. The narrator seems to think that the king is a person with unlimited power.

We can find several clues showing that the king is a serious ruler. On a sleepless night he reads the annals, learns about a loyal action of an official (Mordecai) that remains unrecognized, finds the best way to award him (chap. 6, the way Haman himself wanted to be honored), and carries it out right away. He is generous as to offer the loyal official to play a king by allowing him to wear royal robes and a crown and riding on horseback through the open square of the city (6:11). The king reveals his character through words and actions. He is action oriented and quick to respond to a given situation. He is quite able and thus handles everything with his power. The narrator desires what the king is and has: generosity, carelessness, efficiency, confidence, and absolute power, among other things. The king holds people's destinies in his hands. Seeing him as a buffoon blocks the reader from seeing the power in his office and his powerful hands.

What the king is really doing behind his seemingly humorous character is tactfully handling different interest groups. In the event of a racial problem (as presented by Haman) instead of making a policy for all to enjoy well-being and peace, the king goes for elimination of the group. He does it with Haman's group, too. The king just eliminates any turbulence. This way the empire and the emperor lose nothing. The emperor is the one who always wins. Not surprisingly, the last action of the king is letting the people of the land and islands give him tributes (10:1).

Haman

Haman plays an evil role and his anger toward all Jews seems too much. Even scholars who critically analyze the king, Esther, and Mordecai often remain uncritical about Haman's characterization. They take Haman as a plain villain. Bechtel thinks that Haman is not only evil, but also excellent, deceiving, and smart.[15] Bush observes that the narrator directly describes Haman's emotions

---

[15] Bechtel, *Esther*, 80.

and feelings: anger (3:5; 5:9), joy (5:9), sorrow and shame (6:12), fear (7:6), thought (6:6), intention (3:6), and awareness (7:7). He is described as an irrational villain.[16] Haman's motive, driving force, and attitude are transparent and his twisted soul is exposed.[17] For Berlin, Haman is not so evil because he is the archetypal comic villain.[18] So we are not meant to feel threatened by the comic villain. But still in comedy, Haman is an imposter or self-deceiving braggart. In this regard, sometimes scholars are not fair to Haman. Humphreys thinks that Haman's characteristics do not change, remaining evil from the beginning to the end.[19] But this is not true. Haman did not oppress Mordecai or the Jews before Mordecai caused the problem.

I believe that all major characters, including Esther and Mordecai, are dangerous and evil. Haman seems to be another face of Mordecai and the narrator. He is now having what Mordecai desperately wants. He is closest to the emperor. Thus he needs to be removed for Mordecai to become the second in command. In the eyes of Mordecai, Haman is high up there enjoying power. But his power is not the absolute power as the king has it. What the narrator ultimately wants is to be like the emperor. That is why Mordecai ignores Haman. Getting rid of Haman is not the ultimate goal. He happens to be there on the way to the emperor. So the conflict with him is necessary. Getting victory over the conflict with Haman and having Haman's house is not equal to being enthroned as the emperor. But Mordecai's wearing the king's clothes and crown, riding on the king's horse, and being paraded around Susa symbolizes taking over the throne. That is the finale of the narrator's fantasy.

Haman dies unjustly. Neither the narrator nor any of the book's characters make reference to his death. Haman's family and his supporters meet the same fate. Attack against Haman is disguised in the name of fortuity, literary reversal, and providence (7:8). The book is not interested in morality. Is Haman really representing evil in the story? Haman is also like Mordecai who is in a survival game. Who is really greedy and evil in the story? All the major characters are!

The book does not explain the real reason why Mordecai does not bow to Haman. Instead, the narrator mentions briefly the ancestral backgrounds of Haman and Mordecai. Haman is the Agagite (3:1) and Mordecai is the Benjaminite (2:5). Scholars are too kind and do not trace the causes of this enmity all the way back to the war between their possible ancestors, King Saul and King Agag of the Amalekites (I Sam 15). For Fox, it shows that Haman's anti-Semitic attitude did not come from racial or religious hatred.[20] This kind of

---

[16] Bush, *Ruth, Esther*, 495–6.

[17] Michael Fox, "The Structure of the Book of Esther," In Isaac Leo Seligmann Volume, *Essays on the Bible and the Ancient World*, ed. A. Rofe and Y. Zakovitch. (Jerusalem: Rubinstein, 1983), 178.

[18] Berlin, *Esther*, xx.

[19] Lee Humphreys, "A Life-Style for Diaspora: A Study of the Tales of Esther and Daniel," *JBL* 92 (1973): 107–8.

[20] Fox, "The Structure of the Book of Esther," 181.

rationalization finds the cause of the conflict between two men in the long enmity between the tribes. But the narrator never says that.

It is true that Haman is the opposite of Mordecai in the story. Haman may not be evil, but represents a major hurdle for Mordecai to go up the social ladder. Mordecai's enemy is not the Persians, but Haman and his group, another ethnic minority group. In the end, Haman, his family, eight hundred citizens of Susa, and 75,000 people outside the city are destroyed. The story seems to teach that within the empire ethnic minority groups can have conflicts with each other but they are not to touch the empire itself. It is the foundation of the empire.

Esther

Esther and Vashti represent the narrator's desire for the opposite sex. So the two function as one, namely, the category of women. The beauty of these women is out of this place. They represent every man's dream woman. It seems for the narrator that if any powerful and rich man does not have a woman like these, he would not be considered as truly successful.

Scholars often think that Esther's character develops from passive to active and even strategic as the crisis unfolds.[21] I believe that this character change also has to do with the changes in the desire of the narrator. The narrator desires Esther, but she becomes the king's woman. She is not available to anyone else. Desiring Esther's sex is expressed through Haman's (un)attempt when he "throws himself on the couch where Esther was reclining" to seek to save his life (7:8). His attempt to have her should fail. The narrator would not allow it. That is why the king judges Haman's action as an attempted rape. Fittingly, Haman ends up hung on a high pole, a symbol of the phallus. In fact, the narrator also blocks Esther "to go into the king" anymore, since the beauty selection scene (chap. 2). She "appears" before the king but never "goes into the king."

Contra to the suggestion that Mordecai could take her as his wife,[22] I maintain that he cannot take her as his wife. It seems better for Mordecai to give up sex and rather to have power and honor. Esther had better stay close to the king for Mordecai's use at the opportune time. Without her, Mordecai would not have any means to the place of his ultimate desire, the throne. Initially, the narrator desired sex, too. But as Vashti's refusal symbolizes, the narrator learns that "You cannot have it all." So Esther should become a means for a greedy man to achieve his goal. Esther's speech, "If I perish, I perish," (4:16) is the turning point where she is given up as a sex object and is reborn as the incarnation of Mordecai's avarice and revenge. She now has to do whatever the man directs. The true character change for Esther is from that of a potential sex

---

[21] Humphreys, "A Life-Style for Diaspora," 106; Bush, *Ruth, Esther,* 498–550.
[22] In LXX 2.7 Mordecai takes Esther for a wife.

object or sex fantasy to a useful woman conspirator. In taking the latter role, she becomes violent, crafty, cruel, and fatal. She says to the king, "If it pleases the king, let the Jews who are in Susa be allowed tomorrow also to do according to this day's edict, and let the ten sons of Haman be hanged on the gallows." (9:13) The king did not think of hanging the already dead ten sons of Haman. She is the embodiment of Mordecai's anger and jealousy. Thus Esther becomes the most violent character.

The more violent and cruel Esther gets, the more access Mordecai has to get higher and closer to the king. He finally enjoys seeing the king face to face and receives the royal ring (8:15). Previously when Mordecai was rewarded with royal robes, horse, crown, and parade there was no face to face encounter with the king. This time Mordecai "comes out from the presence of the king, wearing royal robes of blue and white, with a great golden crown and a mantle of fine linen and purple" and the city of Susa shouts and rejoices (8:15). He becomes a king in a way. In the rest of the book Ahasuerus appears only once to give more permission to kill the enemies of the Jews. Mordecai takes over, becomes a subject of many active verbs, functions like a king, and is honored the most.

In the beginning Esther is an innocent young girl and follows her uncle's direction. She is fearful of appearing before the king. She is also principle-oriented, trying not to violate the court protocol. Once she becomes the queen, she is able to say no (to Mordecai's request, 4:8). The man gets furious because he sees Vashti in Esther. So he threatens her (4:13–14). Haman is not the only one who is revenged. Since Esther is not available, she is to be revenged just like Vashti. There is no reward for Esther. There is no material or honorary reward. It is Mordecai who is given Haman's house, royal robes, crown, horse, public parade, and the final recognition recorded in the king's annals (10:2). Esther gets to enjoy only the empty words of the king several times, offering of "the half of the kingdom." There is no appreciation, no recognition whether it is from Mordecai, the Jews, or the narrator. Esther's last speech and appearance is when she asks the king to kill the enemies of the Jews "tomorrow again" (9:13). What revenge!

Mordecai

Scholars say that Mordecai is the most ambiguous character. Above all, his motive not to bow to Haman is unclear. When he is seen as an ideal Diaspora Jew or a model of a wise courtier, his motive remains unclear.[23] For us, his motive is clear and very humane. Mordecai is the embodiment of the narrator's desires. As readers, scholars tend to defend and justify Mordecai's actions. But he is the one who created the problem. He did not bow to Haman and violated the King's command repeatedly and stubbornly until Haman could not take it anymore. Mordecai did not listen to his colleagues' warning. Whether he was

---

[23] Bush, *Ruth, Esther*, 497; Berlin, *Esther*, xx.

jealous of Haman or if he was immature, he is the very one who brought the crisis upon his own people. Bush points out that both Esther and Mordecai are immoral.[24] This moral failure is the narrator's failure. He enjoys the fantasy of violating morality freely.

Mordecai can be charged with the following counts:
1. He made a young niece a sex worker by sending her to the harem. We may ask if he would have done it if she were his own daughter.
2. By his immaturity, jealousy, or whatever reason, he caused a huge crisis for the Jewish community. He never acknowledged nor took responsibility for either.
3. By threat he made Esther risk her life.
4. He made Esther do the dirty work of killing Haman and his supporters, totaling over 75,800 people.
5. Mordecai did not offer a word of appreciation to Esther.
6. He even made his fellow Jews murderers and brought fear in the land (chapter 9).

The narrator does not hide his interest in money. Haman offers bribery money to persuade the king to issue the decree to eliminate all Jews, although the king turns down the financial offer. Somehow Mordecai knows the exact amount and mentions it to Hathach, the messenger of Esther (4:7). In reporting the killing of Haman's ten sons, the narrator adds, "They did not touch the plunder."(9:10, 16) But we know that Mordecai already took Haman's house (8:1–2).

The book of Esther is a dangerous text. The narrator persuades the reader that it is about a story of the weak overcoming oppression or a difficulty caused by the powerful and evil. Here the entire group of Jews, the Agagites, and citizens of Susa are misused. The display of young beauties, the luxurious palace, frequent feasts of delicious and fragrant food, power struggle, speedy development of the story, all allure the reader. The reader is deceived by the juicy literary twists, complicated plot, and intriguing characters.

We have observed that the book is about human desires, especially men's desires of power, material, and sex. The narrator praises, supports, envies, and covets the power of the emperor, material abundance, political influence, and use or support of women. In short, the story serves the interests of the empire. It is a story of a few successful minorities. They enjoy power and material within the system, while they sustain it and sometimes misuse their fellow minority groups to their ends. It is not a story for many minorities and migrant workers. The book does not have a happy ending for at least the 75,800 and more killed, their families and friends, and sensitive readers. Rather, the tragic ending of the book seems to be a warning, a scorn to the empire and human greed.

---

[24] Bush, *Ruth, Esther*, 503–4.

KOREA DESIRES THE EMPIRE

Today's empires are different from the ones in the old days. They do not necessarily go out to conquer others' land. They sit at home, invest money in big development projects in other countries, and exercise influence over the politics and destiny of the nation. Today's empires build factories in other countries, use cheaply their labor force, bring money to home countries, receive migrant workers from other countries, make money at home using their cheap labor, and so on. Korea fits this category and can be an empire.

I am a citizen of that empire and enjoy privileges that migrant workers do not. At the same time, in the future I am affected by all the problems that come from Korea's present inability to create a mature multicultural society. As a child I was taught that Korea is a monoethnic nation. It was a lie. There were other ethnic groups living among Koreans but the government made them invisible. The teachers also taught us that Koreans are the best people in the world. Teaching children to be proud of their nation is not bad. But it runs the risk of making them nationalistic and racist. Even in the very moment of their teaching this ideology, they were discriminating against non-Korean residents living in Korea.

For example, Chinese-Koreans are the ones who have been discriminated against for a long time. They have lived in Korea since the 1880s. They make up more than half of Korea's 1.1 million foreign residents.[25] Most early Chinese migrants came from Shandong province on the east coast of China. Since the establishment of the Korean government after the Japanese colonization the government put strict policies on the Chinese living in Korea. Park Chung Hee who became president through the coup of May 16, 1961, began to implement currency reforms and property restrictions. It ruthlessly harmed the interests of the Chinese community and encouraged an exodus.

With globalization in the 1990s Korea felt the need to invite foreign investments. So in 1998, the government removed property restriction of the Chinese.[26] In 2002, the government started to give green cards to them. Even though they are the third and fourth generations born in Korea, they are not given citizenship, but counted as foreigners living in Korea.

The National Human Rights Commission surveyed seven hundred Chinese living in Korea. Half the respondents answered that they experienced discrimination in public offices and banks, employment opportunities,

---

[25] http://en.wikipedia.org/wiki/Chinese_people_in_Korea_. 71% of those are *Joseonjok*, the People's Republic of China citizens of Korean ethnicity.

[26] They were allowed to have only 660 square meters for housing (one per household) and 165 square meters for business.

promotions, using the Internet, cell phone, and credit cards.[27] So the United Nations Committee on Eradication of Racial Discrimination (CERD) pointed out that the Chinese living in Korea as migrant workers are discriminated against and the Korean constitution does not include an article prohibiting racial discrimination.

Along with the long-time residents of Chinese-Koreans, migrant workers, international students, married migrant women, and refugees, 1.5 million are now making the face of Korea multiracial and multicultural. Among these migrant workers are those who experience the most discrimination. As of 2012 there are an estimated 700,000 workers. Korea is in fact one of the first Asian countries to legally recognize the rights of migrant workers and grant them the same status as Korean workers with equal rights, pay, and benefits. The government started implementing Employment Permit System (EPS) to better protect the rights of migrant workers. But in reality many workers face hardships and abuse. They often work with heavy machinery and dangerous chemicals without sufficient training or protective equipment. They are at a greater risk of industrial accidents, including fatalities, and receive less pay compared to Korean workers.

The Korean government focuses on supporting married migrant women because they become Korean citizens by marrying Korean men. Not just married migrant women, but others also need social services and rights to health, labor, education and other essential services. The Korean government limits the stay of migrant workers to five years. Since Taiwan recently passed the law allowing migrant workers to stay up to twelve years, Korea is pressured to do the same. Korea needs to open doors to families of migrant workers and offer education and social services to them.

The hindrance to peace and prosperity for all comes from all sides: the government, media, and Koreans. Korea is divided into two. Some think that migrant workers took their jobs. Others admit that Koreans are severely discriminating against migrant workers and they lobby for embracing them and all foreigners equally. The media covers murder cases among migrant workers and a migrant worker's murder of Koreans. The media stigmatizes them as a problem and causes division between Koreans and migrant workers. It is a reality that there are many migrant workers who are exploited and inhumanely treated. It is also a reality that there are some crimes committed by migrant workers.

Korea has enjoyed cheap labor from migrant workers but has avoided embracing them. As a result, social problems are coming to the surface. Discrimination and isolation of migrant workers exist in receiving countries around the world and thus social problems rise. The despair and discrimination of migrant workers and their isolation are now expanded to social enmity.

---

[27] http://asiancorrespondent.com/36784/chinese-koreans-feel-discrimination-in-south-korea/ Jul 02, 2010 8:35AM UTC

Behind all this conflict there lies greed. Pursuit of more materials, severe competition, and desires for a materially better life make up Korean society. This drive produces sense of loss, deprivation, the cold treatment of some people, alienation of humanity, etc. Many Koreans are trapped in the game of money, success, and competition. Their desires are about to devour them.

The Korean empire desires more materials at the cost of migrant workers. The empire is the one which invited migrant workers. The empire needs them badly. But it does not make an effort to offer well-being to them. When migrant workers look like a problem, the empire tries to solve it by cracking down and through deportation. The rich and powerful in the empire are the top beneficiaries. They are willing to kill the opposing voices to serve their best interests. Against this background, the book of Esther, which does not have a happy ending, serves as a warning against the empire and human greed.

The prophet Jeremiah advised the exiles to seek peace and prosperity in the foreign city Babylon (Jer 29:7). When the empire prospers, its citizens will also prosper. Peace is another name for prosperity. There was no peace in Susa because the king neglected the conflict between some groups and shut his eyes to the violence among its people. People in the empire seemed to be divided: some were concerned about the creed against the Jews (4:15) and rejoiced when Mordecai was glorified (8:15). Others took part in Haman's plan to destroy the Jews. The Korean government, just like the king in the book of Esther, divides its people and does not come up with a solution for all. The government neglects and alienates migrant workers. It makes policies that meet the needs of corporate companies. People want their empire to prosper. They want what the empire can offer to them. Just like the characters in the book of Esther, people in the twenty-first century Empire are not shy about desiring more money and power. But without making policies good for all and carrying them out, without educating the imperial citizens toward co-existence, the sad conclusion of the book of Esther will be repeated in any modern day empire.

CONCLUSION

We read the book of Esther as a story of explicitly expressing desires of power, material, and sex. We observed how the narrator of the book of Esther supported, praised, envied, and desired power, material abundance, and sex that are available to the emperor, the core of the empire. We also read it as an empire story promoting its interests, rather than a survival story of the suffering minorities. The narrator's desire was disguised in the name of survival of oppressed minorities. We pointed out that the emperor benefited from conflicts among his people and avoided their united rebellion against the empire. The emperor risked or lost nothing. The people did not mind being citizens of the empire either and thus did not try to rebel against it. This kind of story was for a few who made it to the top of the mainstream society and was a fantasy of the narrator.

Then we related this interpretation of the book of Esther to the modern day empire, namely Korea and its dealing with migrant workers in the present time. Just like the emperor of the book of Esther, the Korean government divides its people and takes advantage of the conflict among them. The empire encourages its people to be in the game of power and money so that people do not dream of rebellion. They would rather dream of becoming emperors. The empire and its people are conspirators in the money and power game.

But the ending of the book of Esther reveals the anxiety of the empire. Words like sword, fear, enemies, killing, and striking down filled the ending and block a true happy ending. The fantasy failed. The conclusion of the story warns against the uncontrollable desires of the empire and its people.

BIBLIOGRAPHY

Bechtel, Carol, M. *Esther*. Interpretation. Louisville: Westminster John Knox, 2011.

Berlin, Adele. *Esther: The Traditional Hebrew Text with the New JPS Translation*. Philadelphia: Jewish Publication Society, 2001.

Bush, Frederic William, *Ruth, Esther*. WBC 9. Nashville, Tenn.: Thomas Nelson, 1996. Korean translation by Yiloh Chung. Solomon, Seoul: 2007.

Day, Linda. *Three Faces of a Queen: Characterization in the Book of Esther*. JSOTSup Series 186. Sheffield: Sheffield Academic, 1995.

Fox, Michael. "The Structure of the Book of Esther." Pages 291–303 in *Isaac Leo Seligmann Volume: Essays on the Bible and the Ancient World*. Edited by A. Rofe, and Y. Zakovitch. Jerusalem: Rubinstein, 1983.

Greenstein, Edward. "A Jewish Reading of Esther." Pages 225–43 in *Judaic Perspectives on Ancient Israel*. Edited by Jacob Neusner et al. Philadelphia: Fortress, 1987.

Humphreys, W. Lee. "A Life-Style for Diaspora: A Study of the Tales of Esther and Daniel," *JBL* 92 (1973): 211–23.

Rosenblatt, Naomi Harris. "Portraits in Heroism: Esther and Samson." *BRev* 15:1 (1999): 20–25, 47.

Stern, Elsie R. "Esther and the Politics of Diaspora." *JQR* 100.1 (Winter 2010): 25–53.

White, Sidnie Ann. "Esther: A Feminine Model for Jewish Diaspora." Pages 161–77 in *Gender and Difference in Ancient Israel*. Edited by Peggy L. Day. Minneapolis, Minn.: Fortress, 1989.

http://blog.joins.com/yiyoyong/
http://en.wikipedia.org/wiki/Chinese_people_in_Korea_.
http://asiancorrespondent.com/36784/chinese-koreans-feel-discrimination-in-south-korea/ Jul 02, 2010 8:35AM UTC

THE SAMARITAN WOMAN FROM THE PERSPECTIVE OF A KOREAN DIVORCEE

Chanhee Heo

INTRODUCTION

Much has been said about the changes in thinking and the practical way of doing biblical interpretation. A number of people are reflecting on the new methods and hermeneutics of biblical interpretation based on one's culture and experience, not to be imbued with authority and power, but for liberation.

The story of the Samaritan woman in John 4 has been read as an example of Jesus' mercy and righteous worship in new ways within ethnic, cultural, and feminist studies. Although there are various interpretations, Korean mainstream interpreters have read the text primarily in the framework of patriarchy and imperialism. Therefore, the Samaritan woman is depicted as lustful, dull, and deceitful, whose role in this text is limited to reveal Jesus' amazing grace to the sinner who longs for true worship. Consequently, this paper will reinterpret the Samaritan woman based on feminist postcolonial reading by looking at the story from the perspective of a Korean divorcee, alongside the Korean novel, *My Sweet Home*, by Ji-young Gong. In her book, *In Memory of Her*, Elisabeth Schüssler Fiorenza has pointed out that the oppression of women in the Bible reflects the values of its patriarchal context.[1] In developing her biblical interpretation, she applies four hermeneutical principles, one of which is "hermeneutic of suspicion." Hermeneutics of suspicion raises our awareness about possible androcentric assumptions and positions. Such a hermeneutic allows us to see the biblical story from a women's perspective by questioning the authors' patriarchal context. However, cultural hermeneutics takes a step further and allows us to read the Bible from Korean women's perspective.

Kwok Pui-lan argues that Western hermeneutical reading has assumed universality and infallibility, but it is actually irrelevant to people in other cultural contexts. She proposes a postcolonial approach to enrich and broaden understanding in the local contemporary context, allowing us to read the Samaritan woman from the perspective of a Korean woman's experience. While she thinks that this reading enables us to find how the Bible correlates with Asian women's experience, she also emphasizes "that all feminist interpretations are context-bound. There is no 'value-neutral' feminist interpretation that is applicable to all contexts, and Asian feminists have to find our own principles of interpretation."[2] Kwok Pui-lan suggests "dialogical imagination" in

---

[1] Elisabeth Schüssler Fiorenza, *In Memory of Her: A Feminist Theological Reconstruction of Christian Origins* (New York: Crossroad, 1983), 29.

[2] Kwok Pui-lan, *Introducing Asian Feminist Theology* (New York: Sheffield Academic, 2002), 46.

Discovering the Bible in the Non-Biblical World, which would firstly allow for the use of Asian myths, legends, and stories in biblical reflection, and secondly the use of the social biography of the people as hermeneutical keys to understand both our reality and the message of the Bible.[3] Following this approach, I engage with the novel, *My Sweet Home*, about a divorced woman, to explain the dilemma of a marginalized woman in the Korean context.

SELF-ACTUALIZATION

An organismic theorist, Kurt Goldstein first demonstrated the term self-actualization. He believed self-actualization motivates one to realize one's full potential. Carl Rogers similarly explained this term further by saying that the human being has the tendency to actualize oneself to express one's potential, and to activate all capacities of the organism.[4] That is, the human being is moving toward achieving optimal "human-beingness" for growth and completion with their potential.

Each individual has the potential to realize him or herself. Unless one has pursued one's potential to excel, that is, has actualized oneself, one may not find true contentment and joy in living, have good relationships with others, and contribute to and affect positively the society. That is the reason why those who actualize themselves feel free from others, and they can live doing what they want regardless of social prejudice and cultural control. Self-actualizers judge situations correctly and accept the contradictions of living conditions comfortably. And they accept not only their own human nature, but also that of others. Therefore those who actualize themselves do not feel unnecessary guilt nor do they blame others; instead they contribute to others with mission and purpose. Therefore, self-actualization is a significant process that people should go through to live happily and meaningfully.

According to Rogers, self-actualization is related to an individual's perceived reality and concept of self. This self-concept can be changed by the need for approval by others, which is "positive regard," and it comes from experiencing love, acceptance, and nurturance towards others. Rogers argues that receiving unconditional positive regard is important regardless of conditions of worth that society gives according to one's behavior. When positive regard is conditional, people try to distort themselves to the shape others want. But people who live by this actualizing tendency and receive unconditional positive regard develop "real self." However, if they do not, people grow an "ideal self," which

---

[3] Kwok Pui-lan, *Discovering the Bible in the Non-Biblical World* (New York: Orbis, 1995), 8–19.

[4] Carl Rogers, *On Becoming a Person: A Therapist's View of Psychotherapy* (Boston: Houghton Mifflin, 1961), 350–51.

is not real and unachievable. The gap between real self and ideal self is called incongruity; it leads to anxiety in two ways: denial and distortion of experience.

In other words, Rogers argues that people basically have the desire to actualize themselves, which he calls "actualizing tendency." However, if they do not receive unconditional positive regard from others, that is, if conditional positive regard following social and cultural demands is allowed, they cannot actualize themselves.

Therefore, grounded on Roger's theory, I define a process of self-actualization with these three steps: 1) regarding detection of incongruity between real self and ideal self as "knowing oneself"; 2) perceiving organismic need and one's own actualizing tendency as "accept"; and 3) the characteristics of fully functioning person as the "final figure of self-actualization."

THE SAMARITAN WOMAN

The Samaritan woman in John 4 is an outcast who was divorced five times and suffered from social prejudice and discrimination. While she has a painful life, Jesus seeks her and breaks the social structure which has oppressed her. Therefore, the woman can actualize herself and live as a self-determined disciple who saves many Samaritans in her town.

The Samaritan Woman as Outcast

The Samaritan woman is a marginalized woman whom the society has alienated. Therefore the description of the woman's mental status is a reflection of her outcast status in her society: Samaritan, woman, and having multiple husbands (divorced). By the time of Jesus, relations between the Jews and Samaritans were strained, because Jews thought that Samaritans were not true descendants ethnically or religiously.[5] Both Jews and Samaritan religious leaders taught their people not to associate with and have contact with each other, and they were not even allowed to enter each other's territories. The incident in John 8:48 reflects the typical Jewish-Samaritan hostilities at the time. When the Jews wanted to curse Jesus, they called him demon-possessed and a Samaritan in one breath.[6]

---

[5] The Jews have alienated and rejected the Samaritans for a long time. There had been conflict between the Jews and the Samaritans who were considered as half-breed. After the Assyrian conquest and destruction of the northern kingdom of Israel in 721 BCE, the Assyrians settled foreigners in the land. Those Israelites who had not been deported intermarried with the foreigners. Their descendants served the Israelite God and their own gods in accordance with foreign ways; they became Samaritans (2 Kgs 17:13–34). Reinhard Pummer, "The Samaritans: A Jewish Offshoot or a Pagan Cult?" *BRev* 7 (1991): 22–29, 40.

[6] Wayne A. Brindle, "The Origin and History of the Samaritans," *Grace Theological Journal* 5.1 (1984): 47–75.

And Jews have a demeaning view of women.[7] In Jewish culture, the value of women was defined by their biological function, namely to bear their husbands' offspring. They were commonly considered as unclean.[8] Rabbinic literature expresses misogynistic attitudes toward women; women were described not only as greedy, vain, lazy, and frivolous, but also as evil or nymphomaniacs.[9] This awareness about women is also revealed in John 4. The author of John does not state the reason for the disciples' shock at seeing Jesus talking with the Samaritan woman. But given the cultural context of the time, they would have been surprised with him talking to her since she is a Samaritan woman. Therefore, it was both an ethnic and gender issue.

Furthermore, she has had multiple husbands. In those days, wives could not initiate divorce until their husbands confirmed it. If this woman was divorced five times, five men declared a separation from her and she was abandoned by her husbands five times.[10] Though the grounds for divorce are unclear, it is sure that this woman got a bad reputation by having five men and must have been categorized as a woman who may have been infertile, a bad sexual partner, or adulterous, which would have allowed the villagers to belittle her. Moreover, the man she is living with is not her husband. At minimum, they are not married; at the worst, she is actually sleeping with some other woman's husband. Therefore villagers are likely to treat her as a fornicator or prostitute and their treatment of an adulterous woman might be demeaning and callous. In John 8, the religious leaders demanded the death of the "fornicatress" under the Law of Moses. Adultery was a capital offence in early Israelite history (Lev 20:10, Deut 22:22–24), but the more likely consequence for a woman's adultery in the first century may have been divorce without repayment of the marriage fee (Jer 3:1–20; Ezek 16:35–43; Isa 50:1).[11] In any case, the villagers' treatment of the woman living with an unmarried man might be cold and disdainful.

From these titles ascribed by the society, she would have probably suffered from victim mentality as a Samaritan, a lonely life separated from her community, and guilt with humiliation about having five men as husbands. As soon as she realizes that Jesus is the prophet, the woman asks about right

---

[7] A Jewish male gave thanks that he was not an unbeliever or uncivilized, a woman or a slave. Gerhard Kittel and Gerhard Friedrich, eds. *TDNT*. (trans. Geoffrey W. Bromiley; Grand Rapids: Eerdmans, 1964–76), 777.

[8] James B. Hurley, *Man and Woman in Biblical Perspective* (Grand Rapids: Zondervan, 1991), 69.

[9] Kittel and Friedrich. *TDNT*, 781.

[10] Conversation should not be held with a woman, even though she be one's own. . . . Monogamy was general, but polygamy was still permitted to men. Divorce was allowed on account of a wife's infertility and gave the initiative only to the husband. Kittel and Friedrich, *TDNT*, 777–89.

[11] Ingrid Johanne Moen, "Marriage and Divorce in the Herodian Family: A Case Study of Diversity in Late Second Temple Judaism" (Ph.D. diss., Duke University, 2009), 281.

worship. One crucial difference between Samaritans and Jews was with regard to a worship place: Mount Gerizim or Jerusalem. She might have questioned her religious and racial identity as a Samaritan since she had been discriminated against and wanted to justify herself by clarifying the right place of worship.

And the woman goes along to draw water at about noon, when the heat of the day would have been most unbearable. She is probably well aware of her tarnished reputation and deliberately chooses the least popular time of day to draw water, careful to avoid the whispers, jeers, and clear disgust of her "neighbors." And when Jesus gives her water that anyone who drinks it "will never be thirsty again" (John 4: 14), she might know it would be nonexistent. But nevertheless, the Samaritan woman asks Jesus to give her the water so that she might avoid her neighbors altogether. It is clearly a sad situation of how she must go through her life, afraid of constantly being judged. In particular, the women of the town would meet at a certain time in which they would draw water, but the Samaritan woman cannot participate in the group and share her personal issues with any other people, so her loneliness might have been extreme.

She, moreover, would have probably suffered from guilt. It is relevant here to discuss the grounds for divorce to understand why she would have felt guilt. One possibility is that she was unable to have children. In a culture that placed supreme importance on having children, especially sons, infertility was solid ground for divorce. Another possibility is that her five husbands could have been brothers for whom she was supposed to produce an heir. In other words, all of those who married with her died and she lived with a sixth brother.[12] The last possibility is that she was divorced by husbands for adultery or marital neglect. In those times, rabbis allowed divorce based on the biblically derived criteria for divorce, that is adultery and material neglect (*m. Ket.* 5.5, 6.5; *t. Yev.* 8.5; Exod 21:10–11).[13] Although the reason for her divorce was not clear, sterility and bad reputation were not only humiliating, but also disgraceful for a woman. Therefore, she might feel a sense of guilt and would have blamed herself for the divorces rather than her husbands in this patriarchal culture.

Jesus Meets the Samaritan Woman

It is this woman who has been harassed on account of her social classification that Jesus meets. His meeting is surely not accidental, but inevitable. The

---

[12] The Samaritans reportedly followed a different course, practicing levirate marriage only when the woman was betrothed, rather than married, and the relationship had not been consummated. *New World Encyclopedia Online*, s.v. "Levirate marriage" (http://www.newworldencyclopedia.org/entry/Levirate_Marriage)

[13] Moen, "Marriage and Divorce in the Herodian Family," 272.

purpose of Jesus is not to let her realize her sin, forgive her, and save her. Rather, Jesus tries to make her see and actualize herself in a broken social structure. He needs the Samaritan woman to know who she is, accept it as part of her past as it is, and exert influence on other people as herself.

On his way to Galilee, Jesus "had to go through Samaria (4:4)." The use of "had to" makes clear his intention. Jesus goes to meet her while she is performing her daily mundane chores. The Samaritan woman is not interested in meeting the Messiah or experiencing a miracle, but in leading a quiet life while avoiding her neighbors. So, Jesus chooses his own time and place to encounter her, because if Jesus does not intervene in her daily life intentionally, he wouldn't have an opportunity to meet and talk to her.

And then, Jesus breaks down the social barrier. According to laws and customs, Jesus should be avoiding any form of contamination, but the story reports instead that he talks with the woman and asks her to receive water. It is not only taboo to talk to a Samaritan, it is also improper for a man to talk to a woman except his wife. However, he speaks to a woman in public; not just a woman, but a Samaritan woman, who is twice an outcast in Jewish thought.

Through this meeting, she comes to pay attention to him because of his unusual act and Jesus starts to name her personal facts. He instructs her to call her husband. In their dialogue, the only thing Jesus refers to is about her embarrassing past. Jesus does not highlight her divorced status to humiliate, but to show that he knows about her past despite which he approaches her. By demonstrating his knowledge of her past, Jesus reveals that he is the Messiah who knows about her life, and simultaneously assures her that her past history or present circumstances do not matter.

The Samaritan is initially afraid of meeting with people since she is a shunned woman. However, she finds the courage to speak about Jesus once he acknowledges and speaks to her as a human, not a Samaritan woman, with all that the title implies. As Jesus helps her to realize herself, she becomes an empowered woman, a woman with equal value as any other person and an independent woman, a woman with dignity. The woman migrates from the oppressed past to a self-reliant present so that she is able to reach out to her community with her own voice. She had experienced a marginalized and discriminated life, and she knows how this life as an outsider provides for a distorted image about oneself and leads to distress and loneliness. Therefore, when Jesus helped her recognize the need for self-determination, the woman could find meaning, "salvation," and it enabled her to remind her Samaritan community who were ethnically marginalized from Jews of the need for salvation. For her, the salvation of Jesus was not only the promise of eternal life, but also liberation from a low and alienated life. Jesus knows how a person who understands life from personal experience can influence other's lives and change them.

It was her testimony and her story of self-actualization that led people to Jesus. If Jesus never gave her the opportunity to find her worth, that town would not have been saved. She is the sower and Jesus comes only to reap what she has sown.

TRADITIONAL INTERPRETATION OF THE SAMARITAN WOMAN IN KOREA

Contrary to this interpretation, conservative biblical scholars and ministers who have been influenced by Confucianism in Korea have focused on the woman's identity, rather than on the interaction between the woman and Jesus. Therefore, the Samaritan woman has been described as a sinner: the lying, lustful, foolish, woman. In a book that analyzes fifteen sermons by Korean ministers, the author has observed that ministers regard the reason why she married a long catalogue of men was for the satisfaction of her sexual desire.[14] The woman could not satisfy her sexual life with these five men; whenever she desired another sexual excitement, she changed her husband. To them, the fact that she married more than once indicated her disloyalty to a man, her first husband, which means her lustfulness.

And they regard her as a foolish woman. When Jesus talks about "gift of God and living water" in similitudes to save her, she does not understand what he means. Rather, the woman just demands magical water to save her. They think that she almost loses a great opportunity to receive eternal life forever because of her foolishness. According to Korean thought, women are not as spiritually discerning as men.

She is also considered a liar. Although she has had five husbands and lives with a man, when Jesus requests her to call her husband, she replies she has no husband. They consider her response as an effort to conceal her situation by giving Jesus an answer that is factually truthful, but functionally dishonest. Consequently, the Samaritan woman became a sinner rejected from society, but Jesus visits her to save and give redemption in spite of her past.

These interpretations by Korean scholars and ministers are likely to come from fixed ideas about divorced women and from a combination of unique Korean conditions, Japanese occupation and religions; and from the grafting of Confucian patriarchal culture across the board in Korean society, and to fundamental Christianity.

In the middle of the Joseon Dynasty (1392–1910), nobility who were the governing group wanted their society to be grounded in Neo-Confucianism that not only tried to enhance the ethicality of Confucianism, but also revive clan rules. The nobility created a Confucian hierarchical system for men's sexual

---

[14] This book analyzes sermons of fifteen preachers, totaling 398 pieces, to determine the patriarchal character of the Korean church regardless of denomination after 1985. Institution for Christian Women Peace, ed., *Sermon the Woman Hope: New Sermon, New Church* (Seoul: Pyunghwasa, 1990), 55–56.

desire, and polygamy was allowed.[15] That is, while a woman had to have physical relationship with her husband, a man could engage in sexual intercourse with several women.

In this process, three environmental conditions that suppressed women were formed. First, the notion of Chaste Woman (*Yeol-nyu*) has been born. The nobility made and popularized the notion of a "Chaste Woman" to discipline the sexual dependency of women, and propagated this thought through the book of morality based on "*Samgang*," which contained the basic principles of the practical morality of Confucian ideas. Therefore, women who were cruel to themselves or committed suicide after a husband's death were praised; widow's remarriage was prohibited, and women's remarriage was regarded as adultery.

Second, the meaning of marriage was limited. In Neo-Confucianism, the nation was considered as a magnified form of family. The family was necessary to maintain a nation, and marriage was not an option for woman's happiness, but a duty and measure for carrying on the husband's family line.[16] Thus society did not assign any ideological legal basis for divorce to married women and did not establish the law about divorce.[17] It was impossible to nullify a marriage. Only the standard for woman was created and set and given to the man to justify driving a wife out. And moreover, the society eliminated the legitimacy of remarriage by emphasizing a wife's devotion to her husband and his family[18] and setting negative consequences of the divorce for the married couples.

Third, the role of a woman was minimized. In the Confucian hierarchal system, there was a dominant-subordinate relationship in the family; the wife was under her husband. It was transmitted intact from the patriarchal order of king-subject to husband-wife. So, the nobility ascribed women status and authority derived from family; only men were invested with social and economic rights; family was the best virtue for women. Accordingly, women became child bearers who held domestic reins and swore loyalty to a man, and if women did not follow social standards, they were considered irresponsible and stupid prostitutes.

These repressing social conditions were strengthened during Japanese colonialism. The Imperial government used patriarchy selectively to enforce rule over Korea.[19] Women were important targets of reform and the government emphasized women's education on equal terms with men. It seemed like modern reformation; however, the purpose of education was not for promotion of the

---

[15] Myung-Kwan Kang, *A Birth of Chaste Woman: Patriarchy and Cruel History of Women in Joseon* (Paju: Dolgaege, 2009), 17–19.

[16] Korean Association of Feminist Theology, ed., *Experience of Korean Women* (Seoul: The Christian Literature Society of Korea, 1994)

[17] Martina Deuchler, *Confucian Transformation of Korea: A Study of Society and Ideology* (trans. Lee Hunsang; Seoul: Acanet, 2003), 378.

[18] Ibid., 379.

[19] Korea Women's Studies Institute, *New Women's Study: Korean Society, Women, and Gender*, 76–77.

status of women, but to make them a "good wife and wise mother." It transformed the traditional view of womanhood, one that is suitable for a capitalistic and colonized society, because the Japanese government expected compliant women for colonialism, and submissive colonized people who can be raised by them, namely their sons and daughters. On the one hand, Japanese aggression on a single-race nation enhanced group-oriented consciousness of Koreans. Therefore, Korean society has emphasized a different gender role in patriarchy and demanded that women be exclusively responsible for family, especially childbirth and childcare, and encouraged them to sacrifice themselves. For this reason, a divorced woman was considered to be a person who has given up on being a mother and all these responsibilities in the search for the fulfillment of private desire and due to lack of patience. Divorced women are mothers who ignore their obligations to their children, walk out on them, and disturb their happiness due to their selfishness.

At the end of the Joseon Dynasty (1392–1910), women seemed to be liberated from repression and discrimination through the introduction of fundamental Christianity in Korea by missionaries because it challenged the Confucianism family system and order by permitting monogamy, remarriage, and sitting at table with different gender. However, the combination of customary thought and fundamental doctrines of Christianity led to Christianity becoming just as repressive as Confucianism. Consequently, religious leaders taught that women should be faithful to their duty, fulfilling the roles of mother and wife, idealizing the image of "good wife and wise mother" with maternal calling.[20] And based upon Neo-Confucianism, religious leaders taught that women needed to be prudent in their conduct, emphasizing virginity until marriage based on passages from the Bible.[21] In particular, they gave women strict warning about adultery. When they were translating the English Bible into Korean, they limited the accusation of adultery to women alone. For example, the passage of "You adulterous people" in James 4:3 of the *New International Version* is translated into "adulterous women" in the Korean Bible. Institutionally and legally, these teachings about women have predominated Korean society and produced negative perceptions about divorced women; they were seen as those who are unchaste by virtue of remarriage or having a relationship with another man; that such women betray their family. The prejudice against women has not disappeared and has been reflected in our daily life in the form of long-established social conventions.

---

[20] A woman's calling to a profession was interpreted by religious reformers as God's given mission and the overall "calling" for women was interpreted as that of being mothers. Korean Association of Feminist Theology, *Experience of Korean Women* (Seoul: The Christian Literature Society of Korea, 1994), 204.

[21] They used passages like I Tim 2:8–10 and Heb 13:4 to call women to be prudent and chaste.

MY SWEET HOME

The stigma around the divorced woman is prevalent in Korea as many of the sermons and societal views on divorcees indicate. This prejudice against divorcees is also revealed realistically in the novel, *My Sweet Home*.[22] *My Sweet Home* is Winyung's story: she spends the last of her teenage years with her mother; Winyung grows up to think independently, finding her own dignity through real understanding and love of her mother. Though the novel is primarily about Winyung's experience, I will be focusing on the character development of Ji-young. Ji-young is Winyung's thrice-divorced mother who has children with all her three husbands. Ji-young is a successful and famous author, but she suffers repression because of Korean society's view and attitude toward divorce.

Suffering from Prejudice

Divorced women in Korean society face multiple difficulties and are overwhelmed by a series of problems, but what saddens them most is the prejudice and discrimination.

> I thought committing suicide is better than being divorced twice. It was the problem I had to choose between being shunned by people and being beaten from husband in house.

Even though Korean women can initiate divorce unlike the Samaritan woman, they, like her, face social alienation. Therefore, divorced women cannot but be classified as being promiscuous, irresponsible, and trivial persons in society.

First, a divorced woman who marries another man is considered a flirt. Ji-young married three times and had three children from different husbands. She was labeled a "coquette" by a strange woman. When Ji-young went to her farm in the countryside to visit family with two friends, one of them brought a strange woman. The woman asked Ji-young for a lecture but when she rejected the request, the woman became angry and yelled:

> "You, divorced three times, right? I can understand why you did it."

The woman blamed Ji-young for the divorce, even though her divorce had nothing to do with her refusal to deliver a lecture. And the strange woman attacked her severely, treating her as a person who was interested in tempting every man with her appearance.

---

[22] Ji-young Gong, *My Sweet Home* (Paju: Pureunsoop, 2007.) All quotations from the novel are my own translations.

> "Are you laughing? How can you be unabashed though you are divorced three times?"
>
> "How about marrying and bearing a child again with your comely feature?"

Second, a divorced mother is regarded as being irresponsible to her husband, as well as to child rearing and the family. When Ji-young's son, Doong-bin, fought against one of the mates in his class, his teacher found fault with Ji-young. In the process of explaining the quarrel, the teacher compared the two mothers and took the opponent's side. To the teacher, divorce is evidence of irresponsibility to the child who is raised by a divorced mother; a divorced mother is considered to be insensitive to the child's need due to her work, and the child would not grow up well.

> "You are really famous and busy, so I know you do not have time to care about your son."

However, the opponent child's mother is seen as one who is concerned for the welfare of her family and her child's education. This woman also happened to be the President of the Parent Teacher Association. Therefore, a child raised by such a woman would be good and well mannered.

> "The beaten boy is a model student. His mother is really devoted. ... There is no reason for that boy to fight with others."

One thing to notice here is that divorcees are segregated and oppressed not only by males, but also by those belonging to the same gender. This is similar to the plight of the Samaritan woman who was neglected by her community.

Self-Actualizing

On account of the prejudice against divorced women in Korean society, Ji-young suffered ridicule and discrimination, but after talking with her father, she actualizes herself. Just as the Samaritan woman actualizes herself in the brief discussion with Jesus, Ji-young actualizes herself in three steps: knowing herself, accepting herself, and finding a path to a more meaningful life.

First Step: Knowing herself

Her first marriage was to a man whom she met at university. He participated in demonstrations for democracy and went to prison after a year of marriage. Ji-young worked for a living for herself and her baby, but wanted to be an author as well. So, she wrote a novel and at the time the novel was finished, her husband was released from prison. As her novel was in great demand, she became busy. However, her husband demanded that she should not go out, for her primary role was that of being his wife.

> "I thought his patriarchal thought prevented my freedom, because he shut his mouth with my shout."

After that, Ji-young attempted to write a novel having lived in seclusion. However, she was unable to write a word and decided to sacrifice herself.

> "At that time, I decided to take an easy option.... Cause I thought I would be able to live without the novel."

However, a few years later, Ji-young realized that she could not endure anymore, and sought a divorce. After the first divorce, she realized how she wanted to live, and what she wanted to be. She wanted to be an author and live freely:

> "Sometimes, I wondered if this was real life. However, I should live. I wanted to be an author. Even though it would not give me fame and money, I wanted to express the sky and the wind that I felt."

Her second marriage was to a poor aspiring movie director and right after this marriage she became famous. Her three novels were listed on the bestseller list, but her husband's project was not going too well. Although it was a rare and good fortune to be recognized as an author in Korea, she was not happy.

> "If one person should be going well in a family, I want that to be my husband. He should be successful instead of me."

Dominant-subordinate relationship exists in modern-day families. In other words, wives should be under their husbands and husbands usually accept wives who are inferior since successful wives not only challenge them but threaten the security and happiness of the family. As Ji-young succeeded, violence ensued. In some ways, her literary success justified the abuse. However, it was quite hard on her, and consequently, it drove them into divorce. As Ji-young became famous, her husband's violence worsened, because his violence was provoked by her success. Nevertheless, she did not give up her career. This means that she strived against all odds to realize her dreams. She could not sacrifice herself for her family's happiness; she wanted to live as she desired. Since Ji-young is not the main character, the novel does not focus on the third marriage.

Second and Third Step: Accepting herself and a meaningful life

During her second divorce, Ji-young seems to know, but she did not accept herself. But the dialogue with her father helped her accept herself and change.

Ji-young's parents never rebuked her even once for her divorce. When she decided to divorce her third husband, Ji-young's father called and told her.

> "I do not want you to be a thrice divorced woman, but I hate more to see you unhappy."
> "I know you did your best. Then, stay confident."

In Korean society, divorce is still regarded as a disgrace and brings shame to the family. A daughter's three divorces might be hard to understand and accept for her father. However, Ji-young's father accepted her with all his heart and encouraged her sincerely, and then Ji-young could accept herself and love herself.

Ji-young's change is revealed in relationship with her daughter, Winyung. When Ji-young explained the process of marriage and divorce to Winyung's father to encourage her when she was having difficulties with her stepmother and father, Ji-young emphasized love toward oneself.

> "You do not have to stop loving and respecting yourself. You are not perfect, and I and your father are not. But no one has the right to despise the weakness.... Only the person who loves oneself can love others. I passed my time idly until I began to love myself."

And Ji-young reminded her of the days she has lived, and talked about her life.

> "I do not regret. I think I have no choice to live like that, even if I come back to that moment."

After then, Ji-young tried to find meaning and purpose in her life. The meaningful thing she found was freedom. In all three marriages, Ji-young wanted to live as herself without being bound by the values imposed on women, traditional gender roles, and social and cultural prejudice. She wanted to do her own thing, to express what she felt, and to accept as she thought. Therefore, Ji-young decides to live as an author, writing what she wants, accepting her life and not being bothered by what people say about her, and not repressing her desire for men or dating a man.

> "I married and divorced. And I divorced myself from all the false standards that society enforced on me."

Living meaningfully and with purpose means not only being a person based on the value, but also conveying one's point of view to others. Ji-young thought that the secret of happiness was freedom and wanted her daughter and sons to be happy and free. So Ji-young always stressed the freedom her daughter should have to study in a college of her choice even if it was far from their home. Ji-young did not want to let her go and felt sad about her short stay and departure, but she realized that this was the path that was meaningful for Winyung and respected her choice.

> "I realize that the reason why the Virgin Mary is held in respect is not for giving birth to Messiah, but for leaving her son as he is to die. ... My lovely daughter, go on your way. I will stay here."

Like the Samaritan woman who deviated from social prejudice and discrimination through Jesus' acceptance and lived reasonably and with dignity as a disciple, who lead her marginalized community to Jesus, Ji-young also suffered from her social status as a thrice-divorced woman. Her father embraces her as she is, which helped Ji-young find her autonomy and exert her influence to her children.

However, contrary to her father's response, the Church despises divorce and alienates divorced women. When Ji-young, her daughter, and sons went to a Catholic church, a priest preached a sermon about divorce. The priest regarded a divorced woman as impatient, in other words, an immature person and the root of social problems. He did not preach about drunkards, violent, cheating husbands, but blamed everything on the wife in his example.

> "A woman in the journal endured her husband's incompetence, affair, and violence. And her husband came back to God and her and asked for pardon after forty years, before he died.... We have to emulate the woman.... If she defied her husband and divorced, how would the family be? They would be a broken family, and problem children."

As revealed in the novel and many sermons, a church which professes to follow the teaching of Jesus fails to actually embrace the divorcee as Jesus accepts the Samaritan woman. Many conservative ministers and scholars in Korea regard a divorced woman as a lustful, irresponsible, and insincere sinner who should repent her irrevocable choice for life. Preachers wield great influence on people in church and contribute to the alienation of divorcees and enforce an identity on them as betrayers of God's law, those who bring about failure of faith, and destroy unity.

CONCLUSION

By interacting with the woman, Jesus shows that he visits her not in spite of her past, but because of her past. Jesus does not care about who she is, even if she had multiple husbands and that she lives with a man who is not her husband, and accepts her as she is. Jesus' act was difficult to understand, but the woman could realize herself, take on the important role of a disciple, and lead the Samaritan community to Jesus by his acceptance.

In Korea, divorce still remains a social taboo. Almost all divorced women are the objects of discrimination and prejudice. This social and economic discrimination makes their lives more difficult. As Koreans are increasingly exposed to Western values, many of them try to see the issue from a different perspective, but divorce constrains women's rights and roles as the novel reveals. Mainstream churches in Korea have maintained a contradictory stance for women and have classified and discriminated against divorced women. Even though they should deserve respect as human beings, churches have segregated them from God's love, and have failed to accept them. As both Ji-young's father in the novel and Jesus did, churches in Korea are challenged to be sensitive to identify who the marginalized are in the church and to embrace them.

BIBLIOGRAPHY

Brindle, Wayne A. "The Origin and History of the Samaritans," *Grace Theological Journal* 5.1 (1984): 47–75.

Deuchler, Martina. *Confucian Transformation of Korea: A Study of Society and Ideology*. Translated by Lee Hunsang. Seoul: Acanet, 2003.

Hurley, James B. *Man and Woman in Biblical Perspective*. Grand Rapids: Zondervan, 1991.

Institution for Christian Women Peace, (ed.). *Sermon the Woman Hope: New Sermon, New Church*. Seoul: Pyunghwasa, 1990.

Kang, Myung-kwan. *A Birth of Chaste Woman: Patriarchy and Cruel History of Women in Joseon*. Paju: Dolgaege, 2009.

Kittel, Gerhard, and Gerhard Friedrich, eds. *Theological Dictionary of the New Testament*. Translated by Geoffrey W. Bromiley. Grand Rapids: Eerdmans, 1964–76.

Korea Women's Studies Institute, (ed.). *New Women's Study: Korean Society, Women, and Gender*. Seoul: Dongnyok, 1999.

Korean Association of Feminist Theology, (ed.). *Experience of Korean Women*. Seoul: The Christian Literature Society of Korea, 1994.

Kwok, Pui-lan. *Discovering the Bible in the Non-Biblical World*. New York: Orbis, 1995.

———. *Introducing Asian Feminist Theology*. New York: Sheffield Academic, 2002.

Moen, Ingrid. Johanne. "Marriage and Divorce in the Herodian Family: A Case Study of Diversity in Late Second Temple Judaism." Ph.D. diss., Duke University, 2009.

Pummer, Reinhard. "The Samaritans A Jewish Offshoot or a Pagan Cult?" *BRev* 7 (October 1991): 22–29, 40.

Rogers, Carl. *On Becoming a Person: A Therapist's View of Psychotherapy*. Boston: Houghton Mifflin, 1961.

Schüssler Fiorenza, Elisabeth. *In Memory of Her: A Feminist Theological Reconstruction of Christian Origins*. New York: Crossroad, 1994.

Website
http://www.newworldencyclopedia.org/entry/Levirate_Marriage

RELIGIOUS MIGRATION AND DIASPORA

Hisako Kinukawa

The concept of migration is often discussed in close connection to diaspora. It is perhaps true that by leaving a society within which a person's identity was shaped and going into another society whose mores are unfamiliar, she becomes an "other." By moving she loses her home in both societies. Migration often happens under complicated circumstances based upon political, social, and/or economic turbulence. It may seem a simple matter of crossing boundaries, but for an individual it can imply that there is a forceful power at work so that she cannot avoid moving from one place to another mentally as well as physically. She quite often finds herself marginalized in the new circumstance.

Migration may happen for another positive purpose. That can happen when she tries to find her own identity and crosses boundaries (visible or invisible, physical or mental) as a consequence of her own decision. When Japan was impoverished after the defeat of WWII, a number of Japanese migrated to Brazil with the dream of finding a new world.

MY EXPERIENCE OF RELIGIOUS MIGRATION

I have an experience that I might name "religious migration," through which a person experiences becoming diasporic even though she stays in the same society physically.

My affiliation with the Christian church began when I was a first-year college student. It was also my first commitment to the Christian faith as I am not a Christian by birth. Until then my life was happily spent in our multi-religious and multi-cultural society, which is a mixture of Buddhism, Shintoism, Confucianism, and Christianity. My parents raised their children in these interdependently co-existing religious traditions and conventions.

By committing myself to the Christian faith, I consciously migrated from a multi-religiously blessed, but ambiguously focused situation of faith to a Christian faith in which I wanted to search and find my own values of life as well as my own identity as a person.

I have never thought that my religious migration was unsuccessful, but I also have had to find myself as a diaspora in my country, where Christians have never been beyond 1% of the total population. Christians are a minority of the minority there. They may be respected, but not really valued as having a strong voice on political or social issues. Not silenced or voiceless, but unheard and ignored.

My Christian faith was nurtured in a church movement called the Non-church. It was originated by a Japanese man, Kanzo Uchimura, who started this church independently from any established denominations or traditions. One of the characteristics of the Non-church movement is found in a careful reading of original texts in the Bible and applying the good news to contextual situations in Japan. I could have loved the practice if the interpretations and applications were not male-centered. It was painful to stay in the pew with the uncomfortable feeling that was caused by the heavily patriarchal interpretations of the Bible.

MY SECOND RELIGIOUS MIGRATION

My second religious migration took place when I started doing feminist theology and feminist hermeneutics of the texts. Because of my publications in books and journals, I was squeezed out of my non-church church. I was told that my theology was not appropriate. This was a new migration that took place within my religious affiliation. I decided to leave the church and I became free to work ecumenically and beyond denominations. I have found myself belonging to a very minor segment of the Christian faith, which is already a minority of the minority.

This double migration is really a strong punch that I receive in the Christian church. I am made conscious of the fact that I carry "otherness" as I do my hermeneutics on the margins of the church. At the same time the double migration was both inevitable and necessary for me to live as an engaged Christian.

MIGRATION OF THE SYROPHOENICIAN WOMAN

Now I would like to meet the Syrophoenician woman referred to in the gospel of Mark with a question in mind. Was she a migrant? What were her experiences of diaspora? Some scholars say that she was the first gentile woman who joined the Jesus movement. If it were true, she not only physically migrated to a new region but also changed her religion from whatever god(s) she had worshipped. However, a careful reading of the story denies such an interpretation. Many scholars take it as metaphoric. It seems to me the main concern of the story is not in her religious migration, and much less in her physical migration to Galilee.

A Gentile of Syrophoenician Origin

She is introduced as "A Gentile, of Syrophoenician origin."[1] She heard of Jesus, when "Jesus set out and went away to the region of Tyre" (7:24), where she

---

[1] It is very interesting to observe that this is the only place where Mark uses the word "Greek" in his gospel, and no other synoptic gospel writer uses the word at all. In the whole New Testament, the word is used twenty-seven times. Half of these uses are found in Acts and the other half are in Pauline letters. Exceptions are in John 7:35 and

resided. It has also been contested if Jesus actually traveled to the region of Tyre. He might not have been there, but the phrase "region of Tyre" is very significant for the whole story, because the region of Tyre intersected with the region of Galilee, with no clear borders separating the two.[2] We may plausibly deduce that villages of different ethnic groups were intermingled in the hinterlands of Tyre and Galilee. Syrophoenicia, a colonial state of the Roman Empire, reflects the political situation of Jesus' day. She is introduced as ethnically Syrophoenician, and politically and socio-culturally as a Greek/Gentile.

With Her Demon-Possessed Daughter

She comes to him because she has a demon-possessed little daughter. She migrated herself to meet Jesus with a plea for the healing of her little demon-possessed daughter. She migrated with her little daughter from physicians or healers of her region inhabited by Tyrians. Daring to cross the borders of her culture and religion, she shows she is on the verge of a desperate situation with her demon-possessed daughter.

Despite her fervent plea, however, Jesus rebuffed her with unexpectedly harsh words. "Should you allow the children to be fed first, for it is not fair to take the children's food and throw it to the little dogs?" (7:27). He explicitly rejected her migration through the words despising her people as "dogs" and by defending his own people as "children." Failing in migrating herself, she faced a desperate alienation from both sides, Jesus and the Tyrians.

Nevertheless, she was not knocked down by Jesus' rejection. She talked back to him. "Yes, it is so, but, sir, even the dogs under the table eat the children's crumbs" (7:28). She did not want to lose her identity as a woman with a sick child by coming out of Tyre and being denied even by Jesus. So she kept her subordinate stance that she might keep a relationship with him.[3] We learn that gaining a concrete answer for her plea from Jesus was for her a death-and-life issue. She was pushed to the farthest corner of impasse where she is denied even to be a diaspora.

CITY OF TYRE, REGION OF TYRE, AND GALILEE

12:20, and in Col 3:11. In almost all cases the word is used to designate foreigners in contrast to the Jews.

[2] The research on the cultural context and historical situation of the regions of Tyre and Galilee given by Gerd Theissen, *The Gospels in Context: Social and Political History in the Synoptic Tradition.* Translated by Linda Maloney (Minneapolis, Minn.: Fortress, 1991), 61–80; and the recent archaeological research done by Jonathan L. Reed, *Archaeology and the Galilean Jesus: A Re-examination of the Evidence* (Harrisburg, Pa.: Trinity Press International, 2000), 163–64, 185–86, are very helpful.

[3] Kwok Pui-Lan, "Woman, Dogs and Crumbs: Constructing a Post Colonial Discourse," *Discovering the Bible in the Non-Biblical World* (Maryknoll, N.Y.: Orbis, 1995), 74.

As pointed out earlier, the story reflects the political and social circumstances of Jesus' time. At that time, both Galilee and Tyre were part of the territory occupied by the Roman Empire. Their cities and regions were under imperial control and oppressed by colonial politics, despite the fact that the city of Tyre, an island off the coast of the Mediterranean Sea, was one of the wealthiest and most important ports on the coast of the Mediterranean Sea, well known for "its wealth based on metal work, the production of purple dye, and an extensive trade with the whole Mediterranean region."[4] Because the island city of Tyre had very little space for farming, it had to depend on importing agricultural products from Galilee and other places. "The Galilean hinterland and the rural territory belonging to the city of Tyre (partly settled by Jews) were the 'breadbasket' of the metropolis of Tyre."[5]

THE WOMAN FROM THE REGION OF TYRE

We may plausibly say that the woman is from one of the peripheral villages of Tyre, where people's lives are not as easy as the lives of those in the urban city. On the other hand, taking into consideration such a bitter economic relationship between the affluent city of Tyre and exploited Galilee, we can see why Jesus used such bitter words, which may appear so offensive to the woman.[6] Jesus' bitter words would only reflect the humiliating power relationship that Galileans had to endure with respect to urban Tyrians.

The words overtly express the reality of the destitute Galilean peasants and show their resistance against the power exercised by the urban people of Tyre. Jesus' reply could be considered to represent the common feeling of the Galilean peasants toward the wealthy Tyrians whom they viewed as rich and representing the Hellenistic culture.

The woman with her sick girl must have been socially ostracized because of the demon-possession, and therefore lived in the peripheral hinterland of Tyre. Compared to the elites living in the urban Tyre, she must be neither rich nor privileged. That is the reason she could persevere against the harsh words thrown by Jesus.

She had the courage and nerve of a protective mother to hang on to Jesus. If she was alone by herself, she might not come to him. Migrants are quite often with their families to support. When there are minors to take care of, we also see

---

[4] Gerd Theissen, *The Gospels in Context: Social and Political History in the Synoptic Tradition*, 73. Its money was one of the most stable currencies in circulation at this period. This was certainly one reason why the temple treasury in Jerusalem was kept in Tyrian coin, even though this meant accepting the fact that the coins of Tyre depicted the god Melkart.

[5] Ibid., 74.

[6] Mary Ann Tolbert, *Sowing the Gospel: Mark's World in Literary-Historical Perspective* (Minneapolis, Minn.: Fortress, 1989), 185.

an unexpected strength in the power of endurance until the closed door is wrenched open. Should we call this the power of diaspora, which is displayed when she rejects Jesus' denial of her request? Thus we may say the concept of diaspora is not related to her location, but to her state of mind when she is rejected by both societies.

THE WOMAN REQUESTS JESUS TO MIGRATE

Her tenacity enabled her to talk back to Jesus saying, "Yes, it is so, but, Sir, even the dogs under the table eat the children's crumbs" (7:28). First, she migrates to Jesus' side and acknowledges the primacy that the Galilean peasants ought to have. They are under deprivation of food because of the affluent Tyrians. She admits misdistribution under the dominant relationship of the Tyrians over the Galileans. Then she seems to raise a serious question to Jesus: can he totally ignore a sick child while talking about feeding his "children," the "others" of Galilee? She is insisting that Tyrians are not monolithic and she is one of the "others" in the society of Tyre. She asks Jesus to be consistent in giving primacy to the marginalized wherever they are. It seems like she is asking Jesus to migrate to *her* side and see how desperate her situation is. Had she not experienced being the "other" in her society, she would not be able to be as confident as she is in asking Jesus' help. Her tenacity challenges his egalitarian spirit to work regardless of race, sex, and state. She dares him to expand the table fellowship he offers to any and all destitute people.

Jesus responds to her with words that show he fully accepts her request. "For your words, you may go...." (7:29). He affirms her, as if he has learned a new lesson from her as one of the others. She then apparently left the house where she found Jesus and went back to see her daughter in the region of Tyre, and found her daughter cured. It must be at this moment that she realized she was fully accepted by Jesus. Nevertheless it is very ambiguous whether she joined the Jesus movement or if she experienced religious migration. With her daughter cured, the mother may feel very relieved. She and her daughter may have been energized to life by the encounter with Jesus, even though their social conditions may not have changed at all.

If she joined the Jesus movement with her daughter, it could be because she has found an alternate way of living. If she did, she crossed the borders of religion and ethnicity. Thus she experienced religious migration as well as social migration by locating herself in a new social context, even though her being the "other" may not be changed. She might find a new identity as a diaspora and might find herself energized by being in diaspora with her daughter. The above is only imaginable, and not really spelled out in the text.

JESUS BECOMING A DIASPORA

On the other hand it is more reasonable for us to deduce what might happen in Jesus. When he was challenged by the woman who insisted that she and her daughter were also the ones that should be fed because they were marginalized in her society, he changed his attitude as if he learned a new lesson. Her challenge resulted in his crossing the border of ethnicity, which, we may say, made him a diaspora metaphorically, if not physically. It might have been natural as well as expected for him to work within the circle of his people, the Jews. He must have been made aware by her that he needed to be consistent about his concern for the destitute, the sick, and the poor beyond the borders of ethnicity.

He may not have actually gone beyond the political or social border between the two societies, but her challenge showed him his movement has no borders as long as it sticks to the most powerless people. Her request has made him come out of his social location and move into another social location. Thus his migration took place and the migration could not be possible without him becoming a diaspora even in his own social location.

CONCLUSION: JESUS MOVEMENT AS DIASPORA

It may be plausible then to say that people of the Jesus movement are themselves "diasporas" in their society. They belong to a group of minorities that run against the institutional establishment of the time. If one really wants to be a part of Jesus' movement, there is no choice other than by becoming "diasporas." We are not sure if the Syrophoenician woman actually became a member, but she witnesses to the fact that becoming a member of Jesus' movement entails becoming a "diaspora" wherever one is located. She teaches us that we are also invited to struggle to transform the mainstream that is unwilling to accept those who are "others" and become "diasporas."

BIBLIOGRAPHY

Belo, Fernando. *A Materialist Reading of the Gospel of Mark*. New York: Orbis, 1981.

Conrad Wahlberg. Rachel. *Jesus according to a Woman*. New York: Paulist, 1986.

Corley, Kathleen E. *Private Women, Public Meals: Social Conflict in the Synoptic Tradition*. Peabody, Mass.: Hendrickson, 1993.

Kwok, Pui-Lan. "Discovering the Bible in the Non-biblical World." *Semeia* 47 (1989): 25–42.

Meyers, Ched. *Binding the Strong Man: A Political Reading of Mark's Story of Jesus*. New York: Orbis Books, 1988.

O'Day, Gail R. "Surprised by Faith: Jesus and the Canaanite Woman": *List 24* (1989): 290–301.

Reed, Jonathan L. *Archaeology and the Galilean Jesus: A Re-examination of the Evidence*. Harrisburg, Pa.: Trinity Press International, 2000.

Rhoades, David and Donald Michie. *Mark as Story: An Introduction to the Narrative of the Gospel.* Philadelphia: Fortress, 1982.

Ringe, Sharon H. "A Gentile Woman's Story." Pages 65–72 in *Feminist Interpretation of the Bible.* Edited by Letty M. Russell. Philadelphia: Westminster, 1985.

Schüssler Fiorenza, Elisabeth. "A Historical-Rhetorical Reading." *But She Said: Feminist Practice of Biblical Interpretation.* Boston: Beacon, 1992.

———. *In Memory of Her: A Feminist Theological Reconstruction of Christian Origins.* New York: Crossroad, 1983.

Segovia, Fernando. "Toward a Hermeneutics of the Diaspora: A Hermeneutics of Otherness and Engagement." Pages 57–73 in *Reading from This Place*, vol. 1. Edited by Fernando F. Segovia and Mary Ann Tolbert. Minneapolis, Minn,: Fortress, 1995.

Theissen, Gerd. *The Miracle Stories of the Early Christian Tradition.* Edinburgh: T&T Clark, 1983.

———. "The Story of the Syro-Phoenician Woman and the Border Region between Tyre and Galilee." Pages 61–80 in *The Gospels in Context.* Minneapolis, Minn.: Fortress, 1991.

Trible, Phyllis. "Rhetorical Criticism." Pages 244–45 in *Dictionary of Feminist Theologies.* Edited by Letty M. Russell and Shannon Clarkson. Louisville: Westminster John Knox, (1996).

Tolbert, Mary Ann. "Mark." Pages 263–274 in *The Women's Bible Commentary.* Edited by Carol A. Newsom and Sharon Ringe. Louisville: Westminster John Knox, (1992).

CONTRIBUTORS

Chanhee Heo
Master of Divinity Student, Vanderbilt Divinity School,
Nashville, TN, USA

Hisako Kinukawa
Adjunct Professor, Lutheran Theological Seminary, Tokyo, Japan
and Agricultural Theological Seminary, Tokyo, Japan

Yoon Kyung Lee
Assistant Professor of the Old Testament, Department of Christian
Studies, Ewha Womans University, Seoul, Korea

Lin Yan
Associate Professor, School of Art, Shenzhen University,
People's Republic of China

Yani Yoo
Lecturer, Methodist Theological University,
Seoul, Korea

www.ingramcontent.com/pod-product-compliance
Lightning Source LLC
Chambersburg PA
CBHW031243160426
43195CB00009BA/581